Dance of my Life

Dance of my Life

susan alexander

Librario

Published by
Librario Publishing Ltd

ISBN: 1-904440-98-3

Also by the same author - "In the Light of the Rainbow Tree."

Design and typeset by Scotty-Dog Pictures
Printed by Digitalquill

Acknowledgments

It was the winter of 2007 when I finally got around to sorting out my old ballet photographs, a chore I had been putting off for years. Pulling the dining table into the centre of my cottage-sized sitting room, I covered the surface with the battered clippings, faded images and ancient press cuttings which had been stuck into a scrap book by my father over fifty years ago. It is to him, dear James, that I owe my first debt of gratitude. If he had not taken the trouble to preserve these relics of his youngest daughter's career, there would have been little material upon which to base this book. Not that I had any intention of writing one at that time.

It was my handyman who inadvertently ignited the idea that there was a story which needed to be told. Michael Milmoe is a volunteer for the Moray Handyman Service. This wonderful free facility is offered to 'poor, wee, lone pensioners' like myself who are incapable of putting up a shelf or, in my case, changing a light bulb. The bulb in question was a high ceiling light of a new fangled design situated above the table upon which lay my litter of memorabilia. I apologised several times for being in Michael's way (the light had developed complications), and by the end of a frustrating day he eventually asked me what I was doing. I explained that I used to be a ballet dancer. Glancing at my grey hair and fluffy bedroom slippers, Michael looked doubtful. "Show me a photo of you in your prime then", he challenged. I pointed to one of me in Giselle but he didn't seem impressed.

Next day Michael, returning with a transformer for the light, greeted me with "I've looked you up on the internet" and presented me with a print-out of James Monahan's review of the Junior Royal Ballet Company's first season at the Covent Garden Opera House. This included a mention of my London debut in the role of 'Giselle'. Suddenly a light from the past illuminated the faded images on the table in front of me and put into context my tiny part in the history of the Royal Ballet. Thanks to Michael, I knew that I had to write about it.

Then followed long and frequent telephone calls to my old Ballet Company friends, Madeleine White, Valerie Reece and Michael Boulton and my Elmhurst friends, Prue Rodney and Sue Galbraith, all of whom urged me to get on with it. I thank them all for their patience, help and encouragement with special debts of gratitude to Maddy for her invaluable diaries and painstaking proof reading and to Prue for resurrecting 'Giselle' in the form of a master class for her senior ballet students in May. Also a heartfelt 'thank you' to Sir Peter Wright for his immediate response to my letter 'from the blue' and for offering to meet up for a chat about our shared experiences in the ballet. This was to be a joyous reunion, hosted by Michael and Angela Boulton for whose welcome and hospitality on many occasions I am deeply grateful.

New friends too have been a wonderful source of support, notably Sue and Michael Gassaway. Sue's constant enthusiasm for redeeming the ballet part of me resulted in His Majesty's Theatre, Aberdeen, making me a Patron and Mike's help with my commas, and so much more, have helped me to keep believing my story was worth telling.

I am profoundly grateful to my families. To my parents, James and Margaret for encouraging me in the first steps of my ballet career and for their enduring enthusiasm, generosity and love; to my brother, David, and sisters, Ismay and Anne, for housing me and my friends, for supporting me through thick and thin, for always being there for me when I needed them and for tolerating my domestic eccentricities and unconventional lifestyle with such good humour and affection; and to my own daughter, Ali, and son, Adam, for putting up with having a ballet dancer for a mother. It can't have been easy.

Finally, I feel the deepest debt of all to Dame Ninette de Valois who brought something to life in me which has never died. To believe in someone is the greatest gift one human being can give to another. It is a gift of a lifetime. So, 'Thank you, Madam.'

Contents

Introduction

In October 1956 the Sadler's Wells Ballet at Covent Garden and Sadler's Wells Theatre Ballet were integrated under the Royal Charter and became THE ROYAL BALLET. A public announcement to this effect was made on 16 January 1957 and a year later the newly named Royal Ballet Touring Company presented their very first season at the London Opera House. For me, as one of the young dancers who took part, this brought about the most magical moment of my entire life.

But to understand the significance of these events we need to go back to the roots of the two companies. The foundations of the Royal Ballet were laid by Dame Ninette de Valois at Sadler's Wells Theatre in 1931. Her troupe of dancers, at the invitation of Lilian Baylis, founder of the Old Vic Shakespeare and Opera Companies, opened the 1933 season at Sadler's Wells. Dame Ninette's ballet company now took their place as equals with the Opera and were, at that time, more popular than drama. The Islington theatre became known as the home of ballet and many of us who danced there in later years still hold a deep affection for the Wells. Perhaps it is not too fanciful to imagine that the spirit of Mr Sadler's famous wells, bubbling beneath our feet, seeped through the building above and imbued it with the atmosphere of the life-giving waters which gave the theatre its name.

When the Opera House at Covent Garden reopened after the end of the Second World War, Dame Ninette de Valois was invited to launch the season with her renowned production of Sleeping Beauty. With ballerina Margot Fonteyn leading the Sadler's Wells company, British ballet was established as the great art it is today. A smaller company remained at Sadler's Wells Theatre under the directorship of Peggy van Praagh. Establishing its own identity and producing many innovative new works its reputation grew. By 1950 Press reviews stated: 'unlike the senior company at Covent Garden, the Theatre Ballet lives more on its future than its past and has a greater sense of excitement than their elder sister.'

But until the unifying event of the Royal Charter the future of both companies was insecure. Dame Ninette de Valois had seen the need for a new constitution to ensure that the two ballet companies could exist as entities in their own right should the managements of the Opera House or Sadler's Wells Theatre withdraw their support. We owe not only the birth of the Royal Ballet to the extraordinary vision and dedication of their founder, but their continuing life into the present day.

Chapter One

SCHOOL and STUDENT DAYS

It is January 2007 and I am watching a television programme about the Royal Ballet School. It is entitled *Dreams to Reality*. Fifty years ago my dream came true before I had even dreamt it.

In the autumn of 1957, at the age of twenty-one, I danced the role of *Giselle* for the first time while on tour with the Royal Ballet. The following January, the Touring Company gave its first ever season at the Royal Opera House, since its recent merger with the senior Royal Ballet. As I stepped onto that famous stage, where I had recently seen the great Russian ballerina, Galina Ulanova dance *Giselle,* to dance the same role myself, something extraordinary seemed to come alive within me and I was swept beyond the realms of my wildest dreams. James Monahan, the renowned art critic, later the director of the Royal Ballet School, explains, in his article for *Tempo* magazine, that the season was a crucial test for the junior company, because only Covent

Garden could decide whether they were, or were not, worthy of their new status. He concludes the season was deemed a triumphant success but:

'*The performance which settled the question was, without doubt, Susan Alexander's Giselle. Her performance had an extraordinary air of evanescent charm. "Star" quality, that gift which is either natural to a dancer or never to be acquired, belongs abundantly to this girl; the delight of her performance was that we were seeing that quality for the first time, in all its dewy ingenuousness*'.

Now, as I watch the perfect little pupils of the Royal Ballet School on television being taught by a leading ballerina, I am struck that they all have a dream of becoming one themselves. When, at the age of nine, I started learning ballet I had no such dream and had heard of neither the Royal Opera House at Covent Garden nor of the ballet *Giselle*. My home town of Edinburgh seemed a very long way from London in the nineteen forties and my only experience of theatre was the annual pantomime at the King's. I would not have believed that barely ten years later I would be dancing on that very stage myself.

Looking back, I can see that an aptitude for dance and music was in the family genes. I was fortunate to inherit my mother's petite physique, natural turnout and highly arched feet, as well as my father's graceful hands and a love of dance. Both my parents adored ballroom dancing and, as a child, my mother was enchanted by pictures of Anna Pavlova, the legendary Russian ballerina. She somehow got hold of a pair of ballet shoes and heaved herself up on the points of her toes with the aid of two walking sticks and let her imagination do the rest. My maternal grandmother was a passionate pianist as well as being multi-talented with her hands. I remember wonderful tea parties when she would play Chopin Mazurkas and Brahms Waltzes while we children guzzled delectable sponge cakes. Granny's work bag was always full of exquisite embroidery, intricate

4

knitting and a sherry bottle tucked away at the bottom. I have inherited a love for creative sewing and a taste for the occasional sherry but my bottles live discreetly under the kitchen sink.

Performing was also part of family life, whether it was on the ice rink with my father and aunts, who were champion skaters, or musical evenings at home. My two elder sisters and I used to hang over the top floor banisters listening to my mother singing Ivor Novello songs often accompanied by her brother on the violin. In their youth they had formed a musical trio with my grandmother and given recitals in some of the grand Fife houses.

In September 1944, the headmistress of my school, St George's, invited the renowned Edinburgh ballet teacher, Marjorie Middleton, to introduce classical dance classes into the curriculum. The first we girls knew about this interesting innovation was when the weekly gym class was cancelled and, instead, we were instructed to strip to our navy blue knickers, remove our plimsolls and line up against the parallel bars. Miss Middleton proceeded to demonstrate a series of mystifying exercises which we were asked to copy. I found myself strangely excited as I felt my body responding eagerly. I took to the weekly classes as the proverbial duck to water. Ballet opened a door into an unknown and magical world which took me far away from dreaded Latin lessons and the terrifying game of hockey. Up until the day Miss Middleton entered the gym at St George's, I had hated school. I was hopelessly behind in academic terms and disconcertingly out of touch with other children due to a long and unexplained illness which had kept me isolated at home from the age of seven and a half to nine years old. To this day that lost period of my life remains a mystery. All I do know is that the discovery of ballet saved me from a world into which I did not seem to fit at all. But dance was an element in which I immediately felt at home.

It wasn't long before Miss Middleton invited me to attend extra classes at her studio in town and I found myself being trained and entered for the Royal Academy of Dancing examinations. All I remember about examination days are the heated arguments between my mother and nanny as to who should accompany me to the ballet studio. Nanny said, as she took me on the bus from Ravelston Dykes to Palmerston Place twice or even three times a week, then waited an hour in the cold dressing room before returning by the same means AND had to wash, starch and iron my white cotton ballet dress, she should have priority. But my mother was having none of this from a paid employee and so the fights continued to rage on above my head. I don't recall who won but I seemed to sail through all the children's grades without much difficulty. Maybe it was such a relief to get away from the squabbling women that the examination studio felt like a haven of peace!

When I was eleven I won a Royal Academy of Dancing Scholarship. Marjorie Middleton was the chairman of the Scottish Region and on the board of the RAD's Executive Committee for Ballet in Education and her school was the centre for Scottish scholars. Pupils from other ballet schools all over the region auditioned for one of the coveted places. Scholars were entitled to two free classes a week at the leading Edinburgh studio as well as an art class from Teddy Robertson. Mr Robertson's work was widely acclaimed and best known for his gondolier murals in Mackie's Tea Room. Mackie's was THE place to go on Saturday mornings. It became a favourite haunt of my sister Anne and I in our teens because we were guaranteed to bump into at least one of her numerous boyfriends. If I was lucky, I was handed down the ones she'd 'gone off' to be my partners at the Badminton Club Dance. The lovelorn boys were usually still smitten by my glamorous sister and would gaze mournfully over my shoulder, as we trudged round the dance floor, while Anne swept by in another's arms.

I had not attended many scholars' classes before Miss Middleton suggested to my parents that I should try for a place at a full-time vocational ballet school to be trained for a professional career. There was no such place in Scotland so, after much family discussion, a

'Wee Susie' practicing in the garden, Edinburgh 1948

decision was made to enter me for Elmhurst Ballet School in Camberley, Surrey. When my mother and I made the long journey to view the school and for me to audition for a place, the southern county seemed like a foreign country. I was accepted to start the following September and very soon ballet would completely take over my life. No more riding lessons, no more badminton, no more Scottish Country Dancing. Skating was the only recreation allowed as it strengthened the ankles, improved the balance and was good preparation for 'going on point'.

In due course, the extensive and expensive clothes list arrived from Elmhurst and my mother ordered six pairs of grey lisle stockings and my very first suspender belt from Jenners. This Princes Street shop was the Harrods of the North and thought superior to Mackie's for afternoon tea. Two grey woollen skirts (carefully tacked to keep the creased pleats in place), were sent up from the Camberley suppliers along with grey cloak and cardigan and a knitted blue beret.

7

The day came when I left Edinburgh to go to Elmhurst Ballet School, and had to say goodbye to my weeping nanny who had looked after me since I was a baby. As I went up to give her a farewell kiss, Nanny suddenly noticed the strangely inhibited steps of her former charge and future ballet student. The grey woollen skirt seemed unaccountably tight and suddenly we all burst into laughter on discovering the tacks were still firmly in place. Removing the white threads filled in the time nicely and relieved the tension until the guard blew his whistle and the train lumbered out of Waverley Station on its eight-hour journey to London.

Although my mother accompanied me all the way to Elmhurst on this occasion, in future I travelled alone on the sleeper and Ismay, my eldest sister, would see me across London and onto the Camberley train. She was training as a children's nurse at Great Ormond Street Hospital and lived in a hostel in the Cromwell Road. Ismay was also landed with her youngest sister on 'going out Saturdays'. These school exeats invariably followed the same pattern. First stop, the Chocolate

R.A.D. scholar at Marjorie Middleton's ballet School

House in Regent Street, then on to Frederick Freed's shop in Shaftsbury Avenue where my patient sister would wait for hours while I tried on numerous ballet shoes until I found a pair to my satisfaction. Finally we ended up in Ismay's bed sitter where we would attempt (unsuccessfully) to make cheese on toast on the one and only gas ring. We were no more successful when trying to decide what to do after lunch, and by the time we had reached any conclusion it was usually too late to do anything more than set off for Waterloo to catch the train back to Camberley. There was also the question of the one pound note.

This my father always sent me for spending on 'going out Saturdays'. I firmly maintained the money was for my pocket alone while my big sister thought it was for expenses incurred for entertaining her wee sister. To this day we still argue about that one pound!

It was a great relief to be at a school where ballet was the main part of the curriculum (with a minimum of two hours' training every day) but I still got into trouble. Not, as at St George's, for failing to complete my homework, but for asking the wrong questions at the wrong time. Elmhurst was a highly religious establishment and for a child brought up in the Scottish Kirk, many of the doctrines and traditions were bewildering. When I questioned the meaning of transubstantiation in a scripture class I was given a severe reprimand and my refusal to take confession before confirmation was seen as further proof of my heretical tendencies. My Scottish accent was another source of teasing but however much I tried to sound and behave like the English girls, I always felt different. But I threw myself into the ballet classes with enthusiasm and worked hard to strengthen my technique and rectify my faults. My short neck and square shoulders were problematic. I tried to lengthen the former and pull down the latter by trudging round and round the studio carrying a heavy suitcase in each hand but I think I only succeeded in developing my biceps and lengthening my arms!

Despite these defects, I managed to pass the three major exams at the Royal Academy of Dancing in Holland Park, London, including the coveted Advanced. But even this achievement was marred by my failure to give my ballet teacher a thank you present. Why was it that I never seemed to know what everyone else knew was 'the done thing'? I was often totally unaware of what I had done to offend the touchy and complicated teachers. Once I read on the notice board, to my dismay and utter astonishment, that 'Susan Alexander is banned from watching Sunday evening television for the rest of the term'. When I asked my housemistress, 'Why?' her only comment was that I was the most unpopular girl in the house. I still have no idea why I

The Elmhurst Show. Author bottom left

was thought to deserve such a severe punishment as no explanation was ever given.

Elmhurst was a school of favourites and I certainly wasn't one. The only member of staff I felt comfortable with was Miss Milestone. She and Miss Fisher were the principal ballet teachers and I owe much to their skill and training. I felt intimidated by the strict Miss Fisher, but I was in awe of her poignantly beautiful voice when she sang in chapel on Sundays asking the Lord to take away our sins. I seemed to have acquired many at this school. Miss Milestone's beauty lay in her face. Her serene and gentle features, framed by a halo of glossy ebony hair, made her ideally suited to the role of the Madonna which she took every year in the Christmas play. I sensed the kindness of spirit Miss Milestone portrayed came from her heart and it was from this lovely lady I drew comfort and encouragement.

Despite my unpopularity, I did make two lifelong friends at Elmhurst. Sue was a day girl and I was first attracted to her by the

The Elmhurst Show. Author far right

chocolate spread sandwiches she brought every day in a neat little tin. I was delighted to share a desk with Sue especially when she generously allowed me, the starving boarder, to share her sandwiches. When Latin or Scripture lessons got unbearably boring I would open up the lid of my desk in the pretence of searching for something, like a pencil, and nudge Sue to pass the tin out of which I hastily grabbed, then munched, one of the white squares of bread with the delectable brown filling. This ploy worked well until the day, instead of the sweet taste of chocolate, my tongue was shocked by the strong, beefy taste of marmite. A loud 'ugh' alerted the teacher and my secret feasting was discovered.

Sue's parents lived in a lovely old lodge on the river Thames at Staines. I often went to stay with them for half-term breaks. One weekend in December was spent helping the Galbraiths to decorate their huge Christmas tree with special finishing tinsel touches by Sue's father. The magnificent tree was a revelation to me as Christmas at home in Scotland was a sombre affair when we children were expected to be on our best behaviour at the dinner table in the presence of grandmother and elderly aunts.

Sometimes I went to stay with my other best friend, Prue, whose family lived in a big rambling house in the Hertfordshire countryside. My mother accompanied me to Well House after she had come to see the annual Elmhurst show in the Drill Hall at Camberley. She and Prue's mother took an instant liking to each other, chatting away like old friends whilst making fudge on the kitchen range. Fudge and peppermint lumps were the only things my mother ever made at home as the kitchen was out of bounds except on cook's day off. The Elmhurst shows were the highlight of the school year and we girls were always glad of the opportunity, which extra rehearsals gave us, to miss a few Latin or Geography lessons. I loved the excitement of performances which were always of a very high standard. Original works, devised by the ballet staff and senior pupils, attracted enthusiastic audiences comprised of the local population as well as parents and relations.

At the age of sixteen, Prue and I were among a small group of Elmhurst girls who were allowed to attend Saturday classes at the Sadler's Wells Ballet School in Talgarth Road, London. To our joy, Prue and I were among those chosen by the director, Ninette de Valois, to become full-time students the following September when we left Elmhurst. The question arose as to where I could stay in London. After intensive family discussions and many phone calls it was arranged for me to stay with the mother of Ismay's new husband, Ben. Mrs Davies lived with her daughter and housekeeper in a large, comfortable house in the Hampstead district. It was wonderful for me to have such luxurious 'digs' and kind 'landladies' but I am not sure it was always wonderful for them to have a dizzy ballet student as a lodger. My hours were erratic and I was often late for supper after which I enjoyed soaking for hours in a hot scented bath, which I usually forgot to clean.

Classes at the 'Wells' started early and finished late. I was in Theatre Class which had the purpose of preparing the students to enter one of the Sadler's Wells Companies. That is, if you were lucky enough to be one of the selected few. Our class teacher was the gentle Pamela May. This former ballerina and our other teachers, Ursula Moreton, Ailne Phillips, Gerd Larsen and Harold Turner had all been members of the Company and gave me a taste of professional theatricality for the first time. The curriculum included Character and National Dancing, Classical Mime and Stage Make-Up. Pas de Deux classes, when we linked up with the boys, were particularly popular. I relished learning different skills and loved the freedom of student life. I made friends with another new girl, Jennifer Gay, and I spent many happy weekends staying at the Knightsbridge flat of Jen's granny which soon became a home from home.

Sometimes, the students were able to take minor parts in ballet performances at Covent Garden Opera House and experience 'the real thing'. Prue and I, being the smallest, were chosen to be the negro pages in *Sleeping Beauty*. Dressed in gold pantaloons with feathered turbans crowning our blackened faces, we held the trains of the King and Queen's velvet cloaks and accompanied them on their grand entrance for the christening of their baby daughter; we strutted proudly to the throne and sat at the feet of their Majesties throughout the Prologue and were in awe to watch the professional dancers of Sadler's Wells Ballet at such close quarters. The good fairies enchanted us and Frederick Ashton's wicked Carabosse made us tremble but it was Act One which gave us the greatest thrill.

This was the sixteenth birthday of Princess Aurora, and her Royal parents had invited four noble suitors to meet their daughter. The time had come for the Princess to prepare for marriage. From our 'ringside' position we saw the great ballerinas, Beryl Grey and Moira Shearer dance the famous role and we felt the excitement on stage as the orchestra played the introduction for the famous Rose Adagio. This was the moment of truth for any ballerina and I held my breath as the climax of balances approached. After the final magnificent arabesque, Aurora dashed off a series of brilliant pirouettes and dived into the arms of the principal suitor with an abandon which amazed me. Immediately thunderous applause exploded from the audience and it was all I could do to prevent myself from joining in. Never for the split second of a moment did I imagine I would dance the Sleeping Beauty myself a few years later; such a thing was surely impossible for a small and lowly little page even to dream about.

Chapter Two

JOINING the COMPANY

In the autumn of 1953, barely a year since entering the school, Ninette de Valois (Madam) invited me to join Sadler's Wells Theatre Ballet, as a student member. This was the opportunity all we students longed for and, although it was explained I would have to return to the school after the six-week provincial tour, I hoped this would lead to a permanent place in the Company. I was told I was responsible for finding my own 'digs' and was given an itinerary of the places and dates where the Company would perform. Then I was on my own.

My salary of six guineas a week had to cover the cost of board and lodgings, theatrical make-up, practice clothes, shoe ribbon and bus fares to and from digs, rehearsal hall and theatre. This was my first experience of earning and managing money except, of course, for the 'going out Saturday' one pound note! Elmhurst came to my aid and put me in touch with the Actors' Church Union who provided a list of recommended theatrical digs. I promptly wrote to various landladies in Cardiff, Liverpool, Coventry, Birmingham, Nottingham and Peterborough and in due course, letters arrived back to confirm my bookings. I was informed that the cost for bed, breakfast and a late evening meal after the performance was three guineas. I would have to budget carefully to make ends meet.

The Company had a three-week season at Sadler's Wells Theatre in the beginning of October which gave me the opportunity to attend many of the performances and acclimatise myself with the repertoire for the forthcoming tour. I eagerly looked forward to the day I would join the Company and I duly presented myself at Paddington station for the 'train call' on Sunday 25 October. The journey to Cardiff passed quickly as I got to know some of the corps de ballet members but on arrival, as we dispersed into the dark, dismal town I felt I was stepping into unknown territory. It was only the excited anticipation at the prospect of working with professional dancers next day that kept depression and loneliness at bay.

I had been advised to get to the theatre by the earliest available bus on Monday morning in order to bag a place in the corps de ballet dressing room. This 'place' was much more than a space on a shared dressing table at which to sit and make up for the performance. It was the only opportunity a touring dancer had to establish some personal identity. We went to great lengths to create a mini-home, with colour co-ordinated plastic mat, cream pots, tissues and towels. Some even synchronised their dressing gowns and slippers. On one occasion a soloist asked me if I would exchange my lilac gown for her grey one as it matched her powder puff perfectly. I felt privileged to comply.

Every day started with compulsory class. Girls at ten till eleven thirty followed by a similar boys' session. These were usually taken by the director Peggy Van Praagh. Often I was awed to find myself standing at the barre next to a principal dancer but there was no hierarchy in the rehearsal room. The daily class was a very important ritual for the whole company and each day we would gather together and start from the same shared place. Ballet was like a religion to us. Our focus on the mutual passion of expressing ourselves through dance had drawn us from all walks of life. In class we were absolute equals and even on that very first tour, as a humble student, I was treated like the full members of the remarkable Sadler's Wells Theatre Ballet.

On Mondays class was later in order to give the dancers time to settle into the theatre, the stage staff time to unload costume skips and scenery, and to allow the ballet master, Henry Legerton, time to locate the rehearsal room which had been hired for the week. This was often outside the town centre and I can only imagine the difficulties Henry must have encountered in finding a suitable church or similar hall to accommodate thirty-eight dancers for the week. Often the only available premises were far from ideal with rough or slippery floors, awkward dimensions, lack of changing rooms, and freezing cold. Directions were posted on the theatre notice board along with the weekly cast list. The latter could cause elation, surprise or disappointment according to which roles were allocated to whom. I tagged along with other corps de ballet members to find the bus to the rehearsal room on Monday mornings but for the rest of the week we each set off straight from our own digs. Rehearsals followed class and would often continue for most of the afternoon. I was instructed to understudy all the corps de ballet work and tried to pick up as much as I could by following at the back.

My first parts were a tree in *Blood Wedding*, where I was shrouded in black net from top to toe, and a love sick girl in *Pineapple Poll*, where, disguised as a sailor, all I had to do was walk across the stage with a hat completely obscuring my face. In November, around the time of my eighteenth birthday, I progressed to the role of the mechanical doll in *Coppelia*. In this role I had to sit lifelessly still on the balcony of the old toymaker's house until he wound up an imaginary key in my back. I then performed a sequence of jerky movements with round, unblinking eyes concluding by blowing a kiss to the gullible boy, Franz, standing in the village square below. My mother came down from Edinburgh to Nottingham to see me perform my part in *Coppelia*. The doll was misleadingly called the same as the title of this ballet so I hope she was not disappointed to discover her daughter taking such a minor role. Whatever she felt, my mother treated me as if I was a star with a sumptuous meal at the Black Boy Hotel and a posy of flowers to brighten up my bedroom when I returned to my 'digs'.

Sumptuous meals were a rarity at this time of my life. Normally, after the day's rehearsals there was a break when we searched for some inexpensive cafe like Lyons, to have something sustaining, slimming and cheap to eat before going to the theatre for the evening. We mostly settled for poached egg on toast. Performances started at seven thirty preceded by a warm-up at the portable barres on stage and a placing call to acclimatise us to the varying sizes, shapes, surfaces and rakes of the different theatres. We also needed to allow at least an hour to make up and get into costume so our modest meal was usually a rushed affair.

A ballet dancer's life is undoubtedly a hard one and in the 1950s it was very hard indeed but none of us would have wanted to do anything else. Even today we agree there was something special about those early pre-Royal Ballet days and we would not wish to exchange our experience with the more comfortable life of modern dancers. There was an intangible spirit of adventure which rose above the smell of grease paint, the sound of the orchestra tuning up and the buzz of the audience filling the seats in the auditorium. Waiting in the wings for the performance to begin, I felt swept up in the flowing adrenalin as the dancers practised their steps onstage, checked shoe ribbons, shuffled soles and pointes in the resin box and wished each other 'good luck'. For me, a raw seventeen-year-old, it was magic.

It was difficult to go back to the school in Talgarth Road after the excitement of being with the Company but now there was a rare presence in the classroom, which lifted the daily routine into another realm. The great ballerina Margot Fonteyn was recovering from diphtheria and joined the students in class every day. She was weakened by the long illness and to see our world famous heroine struggling with the gruelling barre exercises, just as we were, was a humbling experience. Fonteyn could so easily have built up her strength in a private studio, but when I got to know her in later years I understood that would not have been in Dame Margot's nature. The dedication to her art and to the Company she led was an inspiring example which I tried to follow.

In March 1954 my chance came to become a full member of Sadler's Wells Theatre Ballet. I was given a year's contract to sign and told to prepare for a three-month tour of South Africa. This was a real leap into the unknown. My mother bought and helped me to pack a large new suitcase. The tweed skirts, thick stockings and woollen jumpers I had taken on the provincial tour were replaced by cotton dresses, cardigans and sandals. Some of the clothes I had made myself, including a fitted, floral frock with matching reversible stole and a white poplin blouse to go with my green dirndl skirt.

The Company left Southampton on 8 April on the Union Castle liner, the *Athlone Castle*, to make the fortnight's sail to Cape Town. I shared a three berth cabin with the second youngest member, Valerie Reece, and a senior soloist Yvonne Cartier who was supposed to keep an eye on us. Yvonne smoked small cigars in a sophisticated fashion which gave me the idea of taking up smoking. Most of us smoked on account of nerves, weight and fashion, and we stocked up on the plentiful supply of duty free Players cigarettes on board. Life on the ocean was a rare opportunity to relax and have fun. Apart from morning class on the top deck there was not much to do except loll around on deckchairs sipping beef tea or, after crossing the equator, licking lime ice cream. We played games like charades and statues and on the return voyage we devised a cabaret which we performed in high heels, sunhats and bathing costumes, much to the delight of our fellow passengers.

Shortly after the *Athlone Castle* docked at Cape Town we were immediately bussed to the airport to catch the plane to Johannesburg. Valerie and I were allocated a twin room in a modest hotel opposite a Coca-Cola sign which flashed the message 'delicious and refreshing' through our window all night long. The result was that we were anything but refreshed by morning. My sleep was further disturbed by the music of the *Coppélia* Mazurka going round and round in my head. I had been elevated to proper dancing on this tour but my memory always failed me at the same place where all the Mazurka dancers surged forwards rather like the Light Brigade. Val was not delighted when I kept waking her up in the middle of the night to ask, 'What comes after the charge?' Little did I dream that I would return to South Africa six years later dancing the principal role of Swanhilda with my name in lights outside the theatre.

The two-month season in Johannesburg was a whirl of excitement and now that I had become a fully active member of the corps de ballet, rehearsals filled most of my time. As well as the three-act ballet of *Coppélia* our repertoire included several short works which made up a triple bill. *Les Sylphides,* the perennial Fokine classic, to Chopin's lovely music was a popular curtain raiser.

One memorable evening, during a performance of this ethereal ballet, a large cockroach emerged from the wings and proceeded to crawl towards the petrified corps de ballet of Sylphs. As we knelt in a perfect circle, with our dresses spilt out over the stage, all eyes swivelled in the direction of the beastie who was making a determined path towards our skirts. But not a muscle twitched and the soloist performing in front of us continued her graceful dance with an air of complete serenity.

The central ballet was usually a challenging dramatic work like Alfred Rodriques' *Blood Wedding* based on the famous Spanish classic by playwright Lorca. My part of a tree required much twiddling on black pointe shoes and much quivering of sinister hand-held branches. John Cranko's *Pineapple Poll* was a great favourite with performers and audiences and never failed as a rousing finale. I had progressed to dancing one of the love-sick girls besotted with the irresistible Captain Belaye. I loved this opportunity to combine acting with dancing and later on when I was given the role of the dashing Captain's dizzy fiancé, Blanche, I was in my element.

It was rare to have a night off and these occasions were usually spent in the theatre, either watching the performance from 'out front' or in the dressing room catching up with washing and darning the toes of our pointe shoes. There was a limited supply of these vital and expensive items and we were expected to make them last as long as possible. I still have nightmares about requesting a new pair of shoes from the ballet mistress only to be told I have used up my quota, and having to use glue to stiffen the worn out pointes. Another familiar nightmare was missing your entrance and suddenly hearing the musical cue blaring over the loudspeaker in the dressing room but not being able to dash up the stone stairs to reach the stage in time. On the rare occasions this happened, the dancers on stage would do their best to cover the gap, but even if the audience did not notice, it was a dreaded and shameful experience which still makes me shudder.

Nights off in Johannesburg were invariably spent at the theatre a few blocks down the road, where Danny Kaye was holding audiences spellbound. Whenever we could we would slip across the road to watch and listen to this delightful man. His gift as a story teller and singer were immeasurably enhanced by his sunny, honey personality and we drooled over darling Danny just like the love-sick girls in *Pineapple Poll*. I asked him to autograph the inside flap of my handbag which gave me a thrill every time I opened it for years to come.

On 14 June the Company travelled by train to Durban to spend the next two weeks performing there. One of the significant advantages of these comparatively long seasons was having a free day on Sundays. We were entranced by the huge beaches and the warm, blue sea and most of us couldn't wait to jump into it. One of the boys,

David Shields, ran through the creamy waves and dived straight to the hidden shingle below, which was much nearer than he had judged. Poor David broke his neck. He was lucky enough to make a full recovery in time but it was a terrible shock for all of us at the time. As well as dancing ourselves we were treated to a very different style of performance by a troupe of Zulu dancers in what looked remarkably like Wellington boots. The passion and energy of the glossy black bodies was unlike any I'd ever seen before but the grass skirts did remind me a little of tutus. Another special outing was to the Valley of a Thousand Hills. Bluey-purple shapes fading into the mist of infinity gave an entirely new perspective to the meaning of space. Britain seemed to shrink into a tiny blob on the map in the face of this vast and majestic country.

Our final weeks in South Africa were spent in Cape Town. By then I knew the *Coppélia* Mazurka so well that I felt I could dance it in my sleep and I was adding new roles to my repertoire. I was delighted to be one of the four little girls in Frederick Ashton's *Rendezvous* clad in white dress, gloves and hat with flowing pink streamers. A contrast to this charming period piece was Alfred Rodriques' *Cafe de Sports,* which had its premiere in Johannesburg. Based on the famous Tour de France bicycle race, this ballet was full of wit and fun. I wore knee-length green pants and a jaunty red beret and revelled in tearing round the stage in mad pursuit of the 'cyclist' ahead of me.

Cape Town stands out in my memory, not just for its breathtaking beauty and wonderful climate, but also because my brother's former girlfriend lived there. Alison had become and remained a friend to all my family since she stayed at our home in Edinburgh. She was now married to a fellow South African and both Alison and her husband, Herbie, took me under their wing while the Ballet Company was in Cape Town. They owned a little beach house at Rondeboch and every Sunday I would join them for marvellous swimming picnics. The rocky pools and crystal clear water reminded me of summer holidays on the East coast of Scotland where I used to delight in practising *jetés*

The dizzy fiancé in Pineapple Poll.

on the wide expanses of Lossiemouth beach. But to be able to don my seersucker costume and bathe without shivering was a pleasure I could not have anticipated.

The fortnight's sail home on the *Edinburgh Castle* gave a welcome opportunity to put up our hard worked feet but, unbeknown to me, senior members of the company were meeting for serious discussion about next season's contracts which were due to be signed shortly after our return to Britain. These experienced dancers were tired of giving eight performances a week and touring for ten months a year on wages that were below those of Sadler's Wells Opera, and a third of some non-subsidised ballet companies. They felt quite justified in asking for a rise of thirty shillings a week. As soon as we were back in London the whole Company was involved in heated meetings. I was advised that the request was supported by the British Actor's Equity and to put my hand up when everyone else did although, for me, seven pounds a week was still a fortune.

Fierce arguments with the directors were still unresolved by the end of our August holidays and the delay in signing our contracts threatened the ballet season's opening in September. In the nick of time the directors agreed to accept arbitration if the dancers would work for existing wages for the next three months. I was hugely relieved that the 'strike' was temporarily averted, as I couldn't bear the thought of the Company being disbanded so soon after I had become a member.

We embarked on a tour of northern England and Scotland and although we did not perform in Edinburgh I was able (between visits to Glasgow and Aberdeen) to spend a weekend at home where I was thoroughly spoiled. It was a welcome relief to have a break from the endless round of theatrical digs, which often left much to be desired. I remember my heart sinking on many occasions on reaching a shabby house in a run-down area of town and my nose wrinkling, to be greeted with the odour of stale cigarette smoke and yesterday's cabbage, on entering the front door. Beds could be lumpy or damp and once during an exceptional winter in Stockton-on-Tees the water froze and I didn't take my thermal vest off all week, even managing cunningly to conceal it under my *Sylphides* costume.

I returned to London on a late train after the Saturday night performance with only one thought in my head. A hot bath. At the time I was lodging in a young ladies' hostel in South Kensington where I had a tiny room under the eaves on the top floor. As most of the other young ladies returned to the hostel, after their secretarial or cooking courses, at an hour when I was beginning work, the water

Cabaret on the Edinburgh Castle *on return from South Africa.*
Author third from right.

was usually cold by the time I got back. But fortune shone on me at the end of that terrible week in Stockton-on-Tees and as I sank into the deepest, hottest bath I dared to run I thanked God for answering my prayer.

Aberdeen was the most northerly point of the tour and even in October the temperature felt distinctly wintry. It was my first visit to the 'granite city' and the famous Frank Matcham theatre, but I did not appreciate the significance of His Majesty's until recently. Half a century after I first graced the boards of the well-trodden stage, a new extension was added to the old building and, as a past performer, I was invited to be a patron. When I go to see the vibrant dancing of the Scottish Ballet and the innovative new choreography of their director, Ashley Page, I am reminded of the spirit of Sadler's Wells Theatre Ballet on those earlier tours. It takes courage, dedication and often stoic endurance to perform night after night with fresh enthusiasm, and the infectious energy generated by such companies of dancers sustained us through many ordeals.

One typical ordeal was the arduous journey from Aberdeen to Sheffield. It took thirteen hours. Breakfast on the Sunday morning was at 5a.m. but after two performances the previous day, I felt too exhausted to eat the 'full Scottish' feast provided by my landlady. Instead, I made do with wrapping the sausages, bacon and a hard boiled egg in a paper napkin to sustain me on the long and tedious train journey to Sheffield. This involved changing trains at Dundee, Edinburgh and Newcastle, with waits at every station. Many of us who were still worried about the Company's unsettled future wondered if we were being punished for our rebellion by being banished to the provinces forever. I was fervently hoping that the December – January season at Sadler's Wells Theatre (my first) would not be cancelled.

Much to the relief of the whole company an agreement was reached after twenty-six days. It was the first time any ballet company had dared to make such a stand and although it was a nerve-wracking experience while it lasted it was considered well worthwhile when the new contracts were finally issued. The senior dancers got a minimum rise of a pound a week but my situation, as a newcomer, had not changed. I would still be on seven pounds a week but could look forward to a rise of two pounds in my third year. Holiday pay for all of us was increased which meant fifty-two weeks at full pay. Although the wages of ballet dancers were still comparatively low (even when I became a principal my weekly pay never rose above twenty pounds, rather less than some of the stage staff), the security of a yearly contract was worth a great deal. During the entire time I was a member of Sadler's Wells Theatre Ballet I always felt the honour and privilege of being a part of this historic company far outweighed the hardships we sometimes had to endure. That feeling has stayed with me over the years and has become a vital part of my life, which continues to influence me in all sorts of ways.

Chapter Three

On TOUR and GALA at SADLER'S WELLS

With the future now secure, the new season at Sadler's Wells Theatre opened in January 1955 but it wasn't long before we would take to the road again. Rehearsals for the forthcoming tour took place every day in the theatre studio. It felt good to be 'at home' again and I was in no hurry to get back to my lonely little room in the South Kensington hostel. I looked forward eagerly to each day and can remember walking down Rosebery Avenue from the Angel Tube Station with a spring in my step and my practice bag slung over my shoulder. A sense of purpose filled my life with energy and enthusiasm and I felt happier than ever before. There was so much to learn and although my technique was getting stronger, I still struggled with pirouettes and beaten steps. The soloists and principals, including Marion Lane, Patricia Miller, Stanley Holden and Donald Britton often helped us younger dancers to master difficulties.

But it was one of our teachers, Errol Addison, who taught me how to turn by concentrating on the music and letting the momentum therein control the pirouettes. This was a breakthrough as far as I was concerned. I can still feel the beat of his favourite William Tell Overture pulsing through my veins and Errol's workman-like voice reverberating, 'and a one and a two and a one, two, three', then as I focussed my eyes and brought my head around to the front exactly on the beat, so my body would miraculously follow. The teacher would grin and give his customary words of approval and encouragement, 'Atta girl, Sue!' and I would grin back and start all over again.

When the next tour began in February I was given my first solo. 'Dawn', in the third act of *Coppélia*, was a new challenge and concluded with a 'menage' of posé turns travelling in a wide circle round the stage. These pirouettes were much more difficult than any I had previously tackled and there was no William Tell to help me. To keep focussed, especially when heading straight for the blinding footlights, stretched my ability to the limit. The only answer was practise, practise, practise. On one occasion, after I had performed 'Dawn' without a mistake and felt the worst was behind me, I stood watching the ballerina, Swanhilda, dance her solo. Suddenly she fell during a particularly demanding sequence and had to retreat into the wings. I was left gazing at the empty stage in horror when I felt a nudge from her partner, Franz, standing next to me. He gave me a little push into the centre and whispered hoarsely, 'Go on, do the posé turns again.'

There was nothing for it but to leap to the rescue and keep going until the ballerina had recovered sufficiently to take to the stage again. By which time I was thoroughly dizzy and somewhat short of breath but at least I had kept myself upright!

I soon learned that a good way to get on in the Company was to be prepared to step into the brink if another dancer was off sick. Touring conditions were harsh and provincial stages often treacherous so injuries were not uncommon. I also became used to ignoring minor ailments, such as septic corns, pulled ligaments and strained muscles. This was before the days when dancing companies travelled with their own physiotherapist, so we just treated ourselves as best we could. Surgical spirit was rubbed on the feet to toughen the skin, and plastered toes squashed into agonising pointe shoes. Many of the girls did themselves permanent damage with home-made slimming aids but there was no one to advise us about diet or health, and anorexia was unheard of. We snacked on raisins, nuts, fruit and cheese during the day, when there wasn't time to pop out for a poached egg, but after the performance we ate ravenously the meals provided by our landladies.

Whenever possible I stayed with friends, often friends of the family. In July 1955 my Royal Marine brother, David, arranged for me and another member of the corps de ballet, Diane Forhan, to stay with his commanding officer at Plymouth. Colonel Eustace Frankie was a great character and made sure his batmen looked after our every need. They looked a little disappointed when we refused bacon and eggs for breakfast and ordered crispbread instead of toast but we did justice to the large pile of ham sandwiches left out for us after we returned from the theatre at night. Colonel Frankie's duties included taking morning parade. Diane and I watched this splendidly drilled performance with admiration seeing that the marines' perfectly formed lines surpassed those of many a corps de ballet. Our jovial host looked impressive in his immaculate uniform but when he came in to join us at breakfast, he would toss off his jacket to reveal a huge rip down the back of his spotless white shirt! We felt much more at ease with this awe-inspiring man after that.

In the autumn of 1955, Sadler's Wells Theatre Ballet was on tour in Ireland. We performed in the city of Dublin several times during my seven years with the Company and I always enjoyed those visits. The Gaiety Theatre was aptly named as there was a lively spirit of brightness about the place and we were invariably given a warm welcome.

First solo, 'Dawn' in Coppélia.

Dame Ninette de Valois seemed to embrace the opportunity to come back to her native land as I remember her coming to Dublin on at least two occasions. 'Madam's' periodic visits to see how her younger company was progressing filled us with apprehension. As the great lady sat watching classes and rehearsals, with one leg intricately entwined around the other, we doubled our efforts to impress. We knew she was 'out front' at performance as well and was on the look out for new talent to promote. Discussions with 'Madam' and our director, Peggy Van Praagh, would follow and with our futures in their hands, a few fervent prayers were directed towards the Almighty.

The tour progressed to Belfast, Liverpool, Leeds and Hull, then up to Scotland again by October. This time we did have a week in Edinburgh at the King's Theatre. There was plenty of room in the tall, stone house in Garscube Terrace and my parents were very pleased when their offer of accommodation was taken up by the ballerina, Rowena Jackson. I was a little apprehensive about having such a senior dancer to stay but her warm friendly manner charmed us all. My sister, Ismay, who had come back to live in Edinburgh with her husband, also had two members of the Company to stay, principal dancer, Michael Boulton and musician, Ralph Mace. Family and friends turned out in force to the performances, including my old teacher, Miss Middleton, who invited me to visit her studio and talk to the

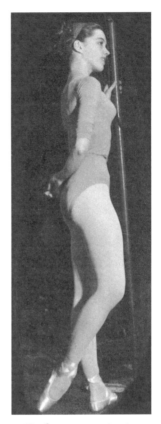

Backstage as a junior soloist.

children about life in the ballet company. Although I had come a long way since leaving my first ballet school, five years ago, I still felt I owed the greatest debt to Marjorie Middleton's faith in me as a little girl.

The Company was given a great send-off at Waverley Station as we boarded the train to Aberdeen. I glowed, in a sense of belonging to both my 'families'. There was no conflict, at this stage, between the one into which I had been born and the closely knit community of dancers who felt like my new brothers and sisters.

On the opening night at His Majesty's Theatre the programme included *Les Patineurs*. Frederick Ashton's delightful creation seemed eminently suitable for a snowy Aberdeen in mid-November. I took the part of one of the 'brown' skaters, descriptively named after the chocolate-coloured velvet jackets we wore over pale blue net skirts. Myerbeer's music was full of charm which the choreography expressed beautifully. During the finalé of the ballet 'snow flakes' gently descended from the flies above the stage. This feat was achieved by two of the stage hands gradually moving a large piece of canvas, filled with polyester chips, backwards and forwards to release the 'snow' onto the dancers below. Suddenly, we found ourselves engulfed by a blinding blizzard and colliding with each other in a manner all too realistic of the weather conditions outside. It transpired that one of the stage hands had been shaking the canvas rather too vigorously causing the other to let go his end. Fortunately the audience seemed to think the chaotic scene was all part of the fun but for us dancers, it was extremely disorientating.

By December we had reached the Tudor town of Chester. Every building seemed to have its whitewashed walls embellished with black timbers and the two-tier shops fascinated me. A wooden staircase ascended from pavement level to a narrow balcony running along the length of the street and giving access to the upper floor establishments. It was not unusual to find a ladies' outfitters, like Jaegers, situated above a Fuller's teashop, where I could indulge in my favourite Walnut layer cake. Sometimes temptation was too great to resist and the strict diet would be conveniently forgotten for a short while. The tour concluded with a return visit to Dublin, presumably by popular request, so we ended up where we started by a very roundabout route indeed.

On 6 January 1956 a Gala performance was given at Sadler's Wells for the twenty-fifth anniversary of its re-opening as a theatre, after years of neglect. In 1931, Lilian Baylis, as director, had produced a

On tour in Edinburgh, with Louise Carley.

programme of opera and drama with members of the Vic-Wells Opera and Shakespeare Companies with Ninette de Valois, 'Choreographist and Prima Ballerina' in charge of the newly formed Opera Ballet. This embryo company of six dancers had grown into the two renowned Sadler's Wells Ballet Companies at Covent Garden and the original Islington theatre, where now we proudly performed in the presence of the President of the Sadler's Wells Foundation, HRH Princess Margaret.

The performance of opera and ballet included several popular arias and the pas de deux from *Swan Lake* danced by Margot Fonteyn and Michael Somes. The Theatre Ballet's contribution was Kenneth Macmillan's new ballet, *Dances Concertantes*. This innovative work demanded great concentration, not only on account of Stravinsky's challenging music, but also because we executed some of the intricate steps perched precariously on the edges of several extremely spindly chairs! The worst part came when, having vacated one's chair to

Les Patineurs with Brenda Bolton, Johaar Mosaval and Shrley Bishop.

dance in complex patterns around the stage, we then had to *bourée* backwards towards the chairs and sit down again in a graceful manner. I dreaded missing my chair and landing on the floor, but during many rehearsals we seemed to develop eyes at the back of our heads.

We also took part in the Circus Scene from the *The Bartered Bride*. The ballet company regularly took the dancing parts in Sadler's Wells Opera productions. Opera nights provided some relief from our own demanding performances, but the long waits until the time of short dance interludes could be very tedious. We had to share the dressing rooms with the opera ladies, some of whom took a fancy to our semi-clad bodies, so we would escape into the corridor where we played childish games of tiddlywinks with make-up brushes and tooth mugs. *Bartered Bride* was a jolly romp full of colour and rousing tunes, but I enjoyed taking the part of the 'dish cloth' hag in the orgy scene in *Faust* even more.

We were soon off on tour again and in March we performed at the Alhambra Theatre in Bradford. I was fortunate that I could stay with my middle sister, recently married and now living in nearby Wakefield. Anne and Martin's ground floor flat had only one bedroom, and the bath, concealed beneath a wooden worktop, was in the kitchen. I slept on the sofa behind the grand piano in the sitting room where I was given breakfast in bed in great style. The bus service between Bradford and Wakefield was notoriously unreliable and often Martin would collect me from the theatre and drive me home clinging onto the back of his Lambretta scooter. This was the first of many happy and hilarious weeks with Anne and Martin and I stayed with them whenever possible.

On 13 April I danced my first Blue Bird pas de deux with Michael Boulton in Southsea. This divertissement from *Sleeping Beauty* was a big step up for me and stretched my ability considerably. Michael was a wonderful partner and his coaching and encouragement helped me to overcome the challenges I faced. The excitement mounted within me as I began to master the steps and my strength and confidence grew. The pas de deux was followed by a virtuoso male solo with a series of athletic leaps made famous by the legendary Nijinsky. Then it was my turn to dance alone. The bird-like solo demanded a darting, dainty style with fluttering arm movements and precise footwork. The whole divertissement concluded with an energetic and lively coda with a series of those infamous posé turns.

Blue Bird became one of my favourite roles, not least because it provided me with my first proper tutu which made me feel a little bit like a real ballerina. Only ballerinas had their own costumes specially made for them. Corps de ballet costumes were shared by many and some of them were years old. Most bodices had several rows of hooks up the back so as to accommodate the varying sizes of dancers and it was not unusual to find the odd patch here and there. But under the spotlights the costumes were restored to the original splendour and, like our heavily made up faces, no one in the audience would be aware of the blemishes hidden from their view.

We returned to London at the end of May for two weeks of performances at Sadler's Wells Theatre. Although these seasons provided a welcome break from touring, it was difficult to find a satisfactory base for such short periods. The hostel in South Kensington was far from ideal and if it hadn't been for the long telephone calls and food parcels, containing treats such as broken brandy snaps or meringues, from my sister Anne, I would have found it very depressing.

In the summer of 1956 an opportunity arose for me to share a small flat in Earl's Court with two friends from my student days. Jennifer Gay and I had become close when we were at the Wells School, three years previously, and used to dream about setting up a little home together. Jen had since joined the Covent Garden Company and become friendly with another young member, Ann Stringer. Ann had recently left the Ballet at the Opera House to teach at the school in Talgarth Road. I was delighted when she and Jen invited me to join them in the mews flat above a garage in Earl's Court. I accepted with speed and alacrity. It was wonderful to be reunited with Jen again and as soon as I moved my few belongings from the hostel and settled into my new accommodation I felt completely at home.

The season at Sadler's Wells Theatre in June 1956 included de Valois' new production of *Coppélia* which was seen for the first time in London. I had now graduated to dancing one of Swanhilda's six friends. The exuberant dance sequences in the first act provided a new opportunity for me to 'dance my head off' (to quote the ballet mistress, Pauline Wadsworth). There were no scary pirouettes in the friends' pas de six and I abandoned my whole self into the utter joy of the dance. It was the first time I remember the exhilarating sense of going beyond my physical limitations into a realm of ecstasy I had not experienced before. In the second act Swanhilda and her friends break into the old toymaker's house and the fun of this ballet reaches its climax. But, as is so often the case, the comedy was tinged with pathos when poor Dr Coppélius's heart is broken and his 'Frankenstein-like' creation is revealed as a lifeless doll. In the third and final act all is forgiven when Swanhilda and Franz are married and the toymaker is presented with a bag of gold as compensation for the damage done by the naughty girls who created havoc in his workshop.

Our programme at the Wells also included another new ballet by the rising young choreographer Kenneth Macmillan. *Solitaire* was a poignantly beautiful work enhanced by Malcolm Arnold's haunting music. The leading role was created for and danced by Margaret Hill on that first performance in 1956. She portrayed the touching loneliness of the central girl with a sincerity and sensitivity which remains alive in my memory to this day. A year or two later, when I danced the role of the Girl myself, I relived the loneliness I had often felt during my schooldays and the feeling of always being on the outside of the established group. There was a tenderness about this ballet which touched me deeply and I loved everything about *Solitaire*: the music, the choreography and the wispy little tutus in soft coral colours and the snug cap of flowers which the Girl wore. The latter inspired a headdress in my own ballet, *Miller's Damsel,* which I choreographed for my Youth Ballet Company on the Isle of Wight twenty-eight years later. I did not realise at the time that those vital experiences of my own youth were building up a wealth of creative material, upon which I would draw throughout my life.

Chapter Four

TWO TRIPS TO SPAIN and
TWENTY- FIRST BIRTHDAY

No sooner had the curtain come down on our last performance at Sadler's Wells Theatre, on 16 June 1956, than we were packing our bags again. There was the usual end-of-week rush to get the scenery, costumes and the travelling skips for the dancer's own belongings loaded into waiting transport lorries. Each member of the Company was allowed a regulation biscuit tin, into which the entire contents of your dressing room 'place' had to be stowed, and a thick canvas pillowcase for practice clothes and shoes. The discipline was strict and there was no room or time for manoeuvre. Sunday was a little more restful than usual because the 'train call' to our next venue was not until the Monday morning. Brighton was only a short journey from London and could be reached by midday but as we were travelling straight to Spain, after a week at the Hippodrome, it felt like the beginning of a new adventure.

On the morning of Sunday 24 June we flew from London to Madrid. There was a coach waiting at the airport to transport the weary dancers to Granada in southern Spain. The journey, through torrential rain, took eleven and a half hours. By the time we reached our destination at 3 o'clock in the morning, we wanted nothing more than to rest our bruised and aching bodies on a flat surface that didn't lurch, bump or jolt. The soft white duvets, in the bedrooms of Hotel Zaida, looked extremely inviting.

Next morning, immediately after breakfast, two smaller local buses collected us from the hotel to take us to the Alhambra Palace. Sadler's Wells Theatre Ballet would perform in the Jardines del Generalife on the following three nights. The weather had cleared and we were able to stretch our cramped legs and ease our stiff bodies with a walk around the famous gardens in the soothing heat of the sun. There was time before rehearsals to explore the fairy-tale magic of this beautiful place and the inspiring setting in which we would dance. But we had yet to see our 'dressing rooms'. Wooden partitions resembling horse boxes, had been erected in the section of the gardens the public did not see. It was the area where compost heaps, garden rubbish and wheel barrows were kept and also the popular residence of hundreds of ants. It proved impossible to keep these inquisitive creatures out of shoes, sandwiches, tights and 'frillies'. These frilly pants were what the girls wore under their long *Swan Lake* tutus and our programme at the Alhambra Gardens opened with the second act of *Swan Lake*. It was even harder to keep still than it had been when a large cockroach had joined us on the stage in Johannesburg but at least he had not invaded our underwear.

The setting of the enchanting gardens gave a real fairy-tale atmosphere to our two performances and thousands of people sat and stood under a star-pierced sky to watch us dance. Gypsies came down from the hillside caves and, keen to entertain us with a sample of Spain's national dancing, invited the ballet company to their encampment at Joaquin after our final show. The atmosphere was electric. Impassioned singing rose to fever pitch as the guitars played faster and faster and dancers' skirts swirled and swooped with flashing speed. Wine flowed, castanets clicked, lightning heels responded with intricate rhythms and supple backs arched like swans' necks as the dancers whirled around a glowing fire. The sultry night sped by and even when we finally got to bed at quarter to six the next morning the intoxicating energy of these fiery Spaniards danced through my dreams.

When the Company returned to London, via the same means as the outward journey, the exhausted dancers disbanded for the annual month's holiday. Although this was our only opportunity to rest most of us attended classes at well-known London studios. We could not afford to get out of training and even when I went home to Edinburgh I kept fit by practising at Miss Middleton's studio and doing stretching exercises in the empty space of my old nursery on the top floor.

We reassembled at the beginning of August for a fortnight of intensive rehearsals. We would not be in London again until the following July, so this was the only period when we could take stock, prepare the forthcoming repertoire, learn new parts and go home to our own beds at night. We would be travelling without a break for the next eleven months.

On 16 August 1956 Sadler's Wells Theatre Ballet and the company orchestra embarked on a second adventurous trip to Spain. This time our destination was the northern town of Santander. Another very long and arduous journey lay ahead. The first part was easy. The Company made the short flight from London to Paris, on a Viscount aeroplane, arriving in the French capital around midday. We were then left to our own devices until it was time to reassemble at Austerlitz Station at 7p.m.

Our main problem was money, or rather the lack of any French currency. I teamed up with Madeleine White and Yvonne English and we decided to walk along Les Invalides to the Champs-Elysees in search of a hotel where we hoped to exchange our pound notes for francs. With the help of a friendly gendarme we found what we were looking for but by this time we were decidedly hungry. Our hesitant French and newly acquired francs managed to purchase a loaf of French bread, some juicy tomatoes, three large peaches and several slices of different kinds of cheese. We ate our delicious picnic sitting on a bench under the trees watching the Parisians as they went about their daily business.

The afternoon passed quickly. We spent the time looking at shops, buying a few souvenirs, strolling by the river Seine and stopping at a couple of cafés where we sipped coffee and smoked cigarettes at little white tables under large white umbrellas on wide, busy pavements. Our explorations were limited because we had to drag our suitcases with us wherever we went but Maddy, Yvonne and I were used to being responsible for our own belongings and much else besides. As a member of the touring Company you had to grow up very fast in some ways, but in others we were extremely naïve. There was no time for boyfriends and we had little experience of 'normal' life. However, in the nineteen fifties, marriage was still a foregone conclusion for most young women and we used to fantasise about our future husbands. Our child-like dreams were usually as unrealistic as the fairy-tale stories of many a ballet.

We succeeded in arriving at Austerlitz Station via bus and metro, in plenty of time to regroup with the rest of the company and to board the overnight train. There were six couchettes to a compartment and after a snack meal in the buffet we were ready to snuggle down for the night. At eight o'clock the following morning the train ground to a halt at Irun on the French/Spanish border where it was necessary to embark with luggage in tow. After another short train journey the bedraggled company clambered onto a coach at San Sebastian. By this time exhaustion reduced most of us into a comatose state and apart from a brief stop at Bilbao, the rest of the journey is obscured from memory. The coach finally reached our destination, Santander, at eleven o'clock at night. Fortunately the entire company was staying at the same hotel and we cheered up as soon as we were ushered into the dining room where a huge spread of appetising food awaited the hungry travellers.

Next morning rehearsals started immediately after breakfast. These took place on an open-air stage, the Plaza Porticado, where the company would perform that evening. The programme included *Giselle* with John Field and Annette Page in the leading roles and *Blood Wedding*. The latter was something of a controversial choice. Lorca, the Spanish playwright, upon whose script the ballet was based, was considered a subversive personality under Franco's restrictive regime and we were not sure how our production would be received. Rehearsals got off to a fiery start. A discarded cigarette, tossed aside by one of the dancers, landed on one of the wooden screens erected at the sides of the stage and set it alight. Fortunately the flames were quickly extinguished before much damage was done but we hoped it wasn't an ominous sign.

We knew all was well when the performance was given a warm reception by the Spanish audience and by the end of the week Sadler's Wells Theatre Ballet had found many enthusiastic fans in Santander. We returned to northern Spain the following spring so perhaps the success of the company's first visit in 1956 had sown a seed for the future.

As soon as we returned to Britain the Company embarked on a fifteen-week tour of the provinces. I was gaining stamina and was now a junior soloist. My new roles included one of the two 'blue girls' in *Les Patineurs,* the dizzy fiancé, Blanche, in *Pineapple Poll* and the waltz in *Les Sylphides.* The variety in the repertoire provided ample opportunity for dramatic interpretation and with eight performances a week we got plenty of practice. Lessons in adaptability and tenacity were an integral part of our lives as there was no option but to overcome the many challenges we faced on tour. One week the stage would be treacherously rough and great care was required not to place the point of a toe in a splintered rut, the next might have a steep rake which caused having to readjust your whole equilibrium, and another could be so small that the corps de ballet needed to reduce the size of their steps to prevent bumping into each other. But there were those theatres, like Stratford-on-Avon where conditions on stage were near perfect (except for one spot, made treacherous by a drop of wax, where many dancers fell). The comfortable green room over looked the river Avon and the dressing rooms were well equipped and spacious. When I became elevated enough to merit the star's backstage accommodation I even had my own en-suite bathroom and a large reclining sofa. I was tempted to cancel my digs and move in!

By the end of autumn we were heading north again and we were in Glasgow when news came that we were to be given a new name. On 31 October 1956 the Royal Charter was graciously granted by Queen Elizabeth the Second to the two Sadler's Wells Ballet Companies, the Sadler's Wells School at Talgarth Road and the recently opened Junior School at White Lodge, Richmond Park. All these establishments had been under the separate managements of The Royal Opera House, Sadler's Wells Foundation and the Governors of Sadler's Wells Trust. Now, this situation would be rectified and there was to be one Royal Ballet Company (with two branches), and one Royal Ballet School (with senior and junior establishments).

I did not realise until recently, that the directors of Sadler's Wells Theatre were under no obligation to house the ballet company any longer than they wished, and it was not until the event of the Royal Charter that our future was secure. Our day-to-day lives did not alter in any significant way and it is only with the benefit of hindsight that I begin to see how my own little life began to play a part in the lead up to the new Royal Ballet Touring Company's first season at the Opera House. Unbeknown to me, Ninette de Valois began to take a keen interest in my progress during the coming year and she was already planning for her Junior Company's debut at Covent Garden.

Since I had danced my first Blue Bird the previous spring, Mr Field had gradually given me more solo work. The contrasting roles of the Betrayed Girl in Ninette de Valois' *Rake's Progress,* the polka in *Façade,* and the white pas de deux in *Les Patineurs* demanded strong characterisation. The tragic fate of the poor girl, whom the Rake had so heartlessly betrayed, was poignantly expressed by the music and choreography and encouraged me to add my own emotion to the part. The saucy polka in *Façade,* Frederick Ashton's witty rendering of William Walton's composition and Edith Sitwell's poetry, was difficult technically but a joy to dance. The White pas de deux was pure serenity and grace and my partner Miro Zolan made it easy to appear to glide effortlessly over the 'ice'. In reality the pale blue floor cloth, which covered the stage to give the impression of a frozen lake, was rather rough and far from easy to dance upon.

Then one day, John Field drew me aside and said, 'Now, I want you to start learning Giselle. 'I do not think I had dreamed of dancing a ballerina role until that moment, and to quote myself from Denis Winton's article in the *Scottish Sphere*, 'I was thrilled but terribly

The waltz in Les Sylphides

46

nervous' at the prospect. I imagined it would be a long time before I actually danced Giselle but I set to work to learn and practise the steps at every opportunity. The ballerina, Anne Heaton took me under her wing and allowed me to attend her rehearsals. I watched every performance with concentrated attention, to absorb the intense emotions of the ballet as well as the choreography. Eventually Mr Field called me to show him what I had learned and rehearsals for *Giselle* began. Alexander Bennet, a fellow Scot from Edinburgh was to take the part of Prince Albrecht and be my partner. From the beginning, there was a rapport between Alex and myself, not just because we shared a name and nationality, but because the sensitivity he brought to his part stirred and softened my heart. The tragic love of the peasant girl for the dashing prince captured my imagination and I tried to find out something about the origins of the ballet.

Giselle is one of the oldest classical ballets and is regarded as a benchmark in any ballerina's career. It was first performed to Adolphe Adam's music in the mid-nineteenth century at the Paris Opera House by Carlotta Grisi. The ballet was a resounding success and is still considered the greatest achievement of the Romantic period. Although the bulk of the dancing was choreographed by the ballet master of the Paris Opera, Jean Corelli, it was Jules Perrot who had discovered and nurtured Carlotta's outstanding talent, and composed all her dances. Mary Clarke, ballet historian and editor of the *Dancing Times* says: 'Therein lies the heart of the ballet'. I had little knowledge of ballet history when I first learned *Giselle* but it was not my attempts to educate myself which influenced me but feeling the heart of the ballet come alive inside me.

It was the fabulous event of the Bolshoi Ballet's first season in London that made the most profound impression on me in providing the opportunity to see one of the greatest Giselles of all time perform on the stage of the Royal Opera House. 'Perform' is not the right word to describe Galina Ulanova's interpretation. From the first magical moment she shyly emerged through the cottage door she WAS Giselle.

47

Immediately, I was swept into a realm of wonder and awe. There was something about this ethereal, light-as-air dancer which filled the atmosphere of the whole theatre and yet, the vulnerability which Ulanova brought to the innocent peasant girl was wholly human. She was ageless, buoyant, ecstatic with an infectious joy of first love, which made the utter devastation of Albrecht's betrayal almost unbearable. The Russian ballerina released something deep within me and I felt that I too would go mad with grief at such a bitter rejection. There was nothing sophisticated or contrived about her performance, nothing held back from those of us who were indelibly affected by the experience. In her own words, Galina Ulanova explains her approach: 'I seek instinctively for that something, that magic language of the dance, which will turn me into Giselle and make me live her tragedy. Then I believe in it so utterly as to make the audience believe in it too'.

I believed.

It was a happy coincidence that the Touring Ballet was in Edinburgh at the time of my twenty-first birthday. My parents offered to give me a party and said I could invite whoever I liked. 'What,' I exclaimed, 'the whole company?' Yes, they would be delighted to welcome all my ballet friends into their home after the evening performance on the twenty-third of November 1956. My 'chocolate spread' friend of Elmhurst days flew up from Staines to share in the fun. It was Sue's first ever flight which added to the excitement and she and I slept in the old nursery on the top floor where we giggled like schoolgirls far into the night.

My father was the managing director of the King George IV whisky distillery in South Queensferry and loved entertaining. His generosity of spirit was well known and he was determined to conduct the occasion in style. 'Pa' arranged, by courtesy of the directors of the Distillers Company Limited, for a fleet of Rolls Royce and Bentley limousines to collect the members of the company from the stage door of the King's Theatre and transport them to number 38 Garscube

The author with Miro Zolan in the White Pas de deux (Les Patineurs).

Terrace. There my mother and Jean, the cook, had prepared a wonderful feast of cold turkey, ham and salmon, with a selection of sumptuous puddings, all laid out on the dining room table. The chairs were pushed to the sides of the large room to leave a space clear for dancing, and cushions had been arranged all the way up the stairs to make an excellent additional seating area. Dancers love to dance and, after food there is nothing they enjoy more, as a relaxation, than letting their hair down on the dance floor. Frank Sinatra and Bing Crosby were my favourite singers and my brother, David, had set up

Galina Ulanova - my heroine and inspiration.

the gramophone while my sisters, Ismay and Anne, had sorted out a good selection of records. My father made sure glasses were kept filled and there was always a wee dram available in the snuggery for those who wanted a break from the dining room 'night club'. It was the most wonderful birthday party of my life and I felt so proud of and grateful to my whole family who extended unlimited hospitality to all my friends.

The next day it was class and rehearsals as usual. In the afternoon there was a pas de deux class at two o'clock. I was one of the girls warming up and waiting for our partners to arrive, and as the minutes ticked by we began to wonder what had happened to them. It was unusual for anyone to be late. Unbeknown to any of us, my father had invited the boys to visit his distillery that morning. Although our contracts allowed the occasional absence from class, to miss a rehearsal was forbidden. No doubt the boys imagined the tour to see how whisky was manufactured would be finished well before lunchtime, but they had not reckoned with the tasting. Many a visitor has regretted his, 'just one wee dram', because, as most Scots know, there is no such thing. By the time the boys finally sauntered into the rehearsal room at ten to three, smoking large cigars and reeking of the famous nectar, it was obvious that one wee dram had lead to several others. Suddenly I was the most popular girl in the company and as my partner, David Shields, lifted me high above his head with reckless abandon I felt on top of the world.

Chapter Five

A PIONEERING TOUR and
FAREWELL at SADLER'S WELLS

By December, Sadler's Wells Theatre Ballet had reached Nottingham
via Stockton-on-Tees and Hull. It seemed a long time since my first
visit to Nottingham, three years ago, at the very beginning of my
professional career. Now, I felt like a seasoned trouper and took the
constant travelling in my stride. I considered myself fortunate in
belonging to this Company which, with eight performances every
week, offered great opportunities for progress. With the distant
prospect ahead of dancing my first ballerina role, I tried to build up
stamina by doing two classes every morning. As soon as the girls
finished at eleven thirty, I joined the boys at the barre to start all over
again. There was something very satisfying about sinking into a deep
plié when my body was already warm and supple, and instead of
their usual creaking stiffness my limbs felt as smooth and soft as
butter. I still start each day with this ritual movement. It requires

Posing with Johaar Mosoval and Michael Boulton.

concentration, calmness of mind and a upright back. As the knees slowly bend and straighten, so the body gently descends and ascends and I feel my equilibrium is restored to the centre of my being. To me, it is the dancer's prayer.

The year ended in Ipswich and the company decided it was time to have a party. The idea had arisen on the train journey from Leicester to Liverpool and, since October 22, every member agreed to contribute half a crown a week. A raffle was organised to raise additional money for which, soloist Sandra Vane, created a beautiful *Petrushka* doll and one of the male dancers, Leslie White made a Fair Isle jumper on his knitting machine. (Lesley did a roaring trade in woollen overtights and leg warmers, essential items in all dancers' practice kit). The mood of enthusiasm grew as party day approached and rehearsals for a cabaret were squeezed into our busy schedule with dressing room doors often bearing 'No Admittance' notices. At last, after the final performance of 1956, make-up tins and kit bags safely stowed in the travelling skips, the entire Company proceeded to Ipswich Unitarian Hall and celebrations began.

Food and drink were the immediate priority and, famished as usual, the dancers soon wolfed down most of the feast they had provided for themselves. Then, well refreshed, we took to the stage again to entertain each other. The cabaret opened with a twenties number, performed by Elaine Thomas, Brenda Bolton and myself, in knee-length thermal vests, flapper fringes and very little else. This perky piece was followed by a play by the stage staff and a couple of satirical sketches with lots of 'in-house' jokes. Miro Zolan and Margaret Knoesen revealed hidden talent with an opera parody, and a saucy striptease by Madeleine White, accompanied on the piano by Errol Addison, concluded the show. The sense of camaraderie and affection we all felt for each other culminated with Santa's arrival (played by director, John Field). We had all drawn a name out of a hat, to decide who would give a present to whom, so the element of surprise added to the fun. Spirits were high and wild dancing to rock and roll records continued well into the night, and what a wonderful night it was indeed.

After a brief Christmas break, the tour progressed relentlessly with very little geographical rhyme or reason. We travelled from Brighton to Stratford-on-Avon, then to the tiny Arts Theatre at Cambridge, back south to Bournemouth, north to Wolverhampton followed by Southampton, Birmingham, Sheffield, Peterborough, Norwich, Southsea, Plymouth and Barcelona. BARCELONA!

Our third trip to Spain in less than a year was to prove a very different experience from either the Alhambra Gardens in Granada or the Santander Festival of the previous summer. The new title of 'The Royal Ballet Touring Company', formerly Sadler's Wells Theatre Ballet was too much of a mouthful for anyone to cope with. The ballet public in Britain was used to the different roles of the Covent Garden Company and ourselves, but the name 'Royal Ballet' abroad meant only one thing, Margot Fonteyn. The English prima ballerina's international reputation generated high expectations of the world famous company she led, and our lesser presence was to cause disappointment and confusion during the coming European tour.

However, the journey to Barcelona, was relatively comfortable and we looked forward to performing at the Gran Teatro del Liceo, with the rare treat of travel-free Sundays. It was a relief not to arrive at the unknown Spanish town in the wee, small hours of the morning, and to be met at the airport by a luxurious coach which took us straight to accommodation booked in advance by the company manager. We had no idea what to expect as this could vary from a modest hotel for the staff and principals to a shabby establishment on the outskirts of town for the junior members. I remember one occasion when our 'lodgings' turned out to be a 'house of ill repute'. We fled to the director to protest and he managed to persuade the manager of his hotel to give us a room for the night until somewhere more suitable was found next day.

In Barcelona, I was lucky. Yvonne English, with whom I had spent the day in Paris on the way to Santander, was my 'digging companion' for the next four weeks. We were put in a little pension in a quiet, residential area, just a short bus ride from the centre of town. Every morning and every night, as we walked through the central street, Los Ramblas, to and from the Teatro, we had to run the gauntlet of whistling youths and fend off pressing invitations to go for coffee, a walk in the park or a ride on their motor scooters. Unaccompanied girls were a rarity in Spain and seemed to give out misleading signals. We felt harassed by these unwelcome attentions but Yvonne and I soon found a delightful chaperone to rescue us.

It was the custom for wealthy patrons of the Gran Teatro del Liceo to have their own boxes, rather like the squire of a village would have his own family pew in the local church. But, unlike an English squire, the Spanish aristocrat, who sat, flanked by his wife and family, in full, flamboyant view of the audience, was also provided with a box for his mistress. The latter was situated on the stage side of the heavy velvet curtain and when this fell at the end of each act, the mistress was obscured from the auditorium. It was a little disconcerting to see these ladies gazing down at us dancers while we warmed up before the performance but we soon became accustomed to their presence and returned their friendly smiles. Yvonne's and my escort was one of these aristocrats and would wave at us from his elevated position, on the right side of the curtain, and throw delicate little bouquets onto the stage when we took our calls at the end of each performance. We could not help being completely charmed by our admirer and he was so dignified and courteous that we trusted him implicitly. Our *gentil homme* (as we christened him), often escorted us back to our pension after treating us to a late night supper, and soon the whistling youths were nowhere to be seen. On Sundays we were invited to visit his villa at Sitges, a popular seaside resort. A car, we were politely informed, would be sent to pick us up from the pension at noon. Casting caution to the wind, we accepted with alacrity, excited at the prospect of a lazy day on the beach. Our admirer plied us with compliments and Spanish specialities which we lapped up with equal enthusiasm. The food was delicious, paella and tiny, wild strawberries were our favourites and the local wine slipped down with amazing ease. I do not remember our benefactor's name but the kindness and respect of this truly gentle man is something I will never forget

Performances at Barcelona's grand theatre were supposed to begin at ten o'clock each evening, but often it was much later as we waited for some dignitary to arrive. The Spaniards do not like to hurry under any circumstances but to rush dinner before an evening's entertainment would be considered a sin. Perhaps they did not realise that the hungry dancers had to wait until well after midnight for their main meal of the day. The only benefit of these late nights was a comparatively late start, as morning class did not begin until midday.

At the end of May the Company took to the road again. We left the elegant city, the seaside villa and the wide, tree-lined streets with some regret. The rest of the tour would not be so easy. There was a

Taking a rest in 'Los Ramblas', Barcelona.

distinct feeling of deja vu as we boarded an old-fashioned Spanish coach, similar to the one which had transported us through thunderstorms and mountains to Granada almost a year ago. The journey to Zaragoza was no less hazardous and there was no time to recover as rehearsals on the stage of the Teatro Iris were called for the following morning. We gave two performances at Zaragoza, and forty-eight hours after we had arrived we piled into the coach once more. This time our destination was the town of Oviedo on the north coast of Spain. The weather had turned cold and windy and

Yvonne English and me with our 'gentil homme'.

conditions were primitive. The venue for performances was the town square where a makeshift stage had been constructed under a flapping marquee. Trying to get changed into flimsy ballet costumes and pink satin shoes behind a screen in a howling gale was quite a challenge. We admired the spectators, wrapped in warm woollen scarves and thick jackets, who stood in the rain to watch us. The enthusiastic applause and cries of 'bravo' were encouraging after the relatively cool reception we had so far received, but it was a relief to find a proper theatre at our next port of call. The three-day visit to Bilbao was our last engagement in Spain. The Coliseo Teatro was an improvement on the marquee but I think exhaustion had set in and my memory has cast a blur over that particular episode.

On June 4 we boarded the overnight train to Cologne in northern Germany. After a very long journey through France, we arrived, feeling rested from many hours sleeping and dozing on our couchettes. We were ready to start work again. Unfortunately, the scenery, which had been disassembled and loaded up on a Spanish lorry after the final performance in Bilbao, was not. Our schedule was tight, with little time for the stage staff to unload and set up the scenery on the new stage before rehearsals for the evening performance began. Consternation grew as there was still no sign of the travelling truck by late afternoon. Rehearsals had to proceed without the stage set which made placing almost impossible. Contingency plans were hastily made in the event of the scenery not arriving in time for the performance but everyone's nerves were on end. Many, too many cigarettes were being smoked and to jangle our nerves still further the smoke alarm suddenly went off. Clad in dressing gowns, with worried faces, half made up and hair half up and half down, the dancers were instructed by a fierce German voice to vacate the theatre at once. While we were standing in a dejected group outside the stage entrance the errant Spanish truck trundled into sight. A huge cheer went up and the valiant stage staff, aided by the resident crew, surpassed their usual efficiency by unloading and setting up the scenery minutes before the curtain was due to rise. Even the German stage hands were impressed.

The city of Cologne and the ultramodern theatre, both newly built since the devastation of the war, were in complete contrast to the more primitive conditions and lackadaisical attitude we had encountered in Spain. Each country had its own character and we learned to adapt to whatever environment we found ourselves having to encounter. After our brief visit to Germany we had an uneventful week in Switzerland performing at the Staadtheater in Zurich. The fresh mountain air blew away any remaining cobwebs and the wonderful Swiss chocolate renewed our energy for the last lap of the long tour.

The final week of the tour was spent in Holland where the original Sadler's Wells Ballet had performed in1940. Their week in the Hague had ended disastrously when the town was attacked by the German army. The gallant dancers, including Margot Fonteyn, Robert

Helpman, Pamela May, Moira Shearer and their director, Ninette de Valois had taken refuge in a remote country house until they could escape on an evacuee ship back to Britain. Now the Dutch, who held a special affection for the brave Sadler's Wells Ballet, had expected to be welcoming back the same company, now crowned in Royal glory. Prices of theatre tickets had risen accordingly and, understandably the audiences felt let down when they were presented with the unknown Touring Company instead. We did our best to win over the Dutch public, during one-night performances in The Hague, Amsterdam, Rotterdam, Utrecht, and by the end of the week when we returned to both The Hague and Amsterdam the response was more enthusiastic.

We finally returned to London at the end of June with just over a week to prepare for another very important season at Sadler's Wells Theatre. We would give our last performance there on 23 July, before the Theatre Ballet was to be united with the senior Sadler's Wells Ballet when both companies were granted the Royal Charter on 31 October 1957. Although this would elevate us to the level of our 'big sister' and give us the honour of having our London seasons at the Royal Opera House in future, there was a feeling of sadness at leaving our theatrical home and the historic name which spelled the birth of British Ballet.

Nearly half a century later when the Royal Ballet celebrated its seventy-fifth birthday at the Royal Opera House in April 2006, the director, Monica Mason paid tribute to the pioneering days of Sadler's Wells Ballet. It was an intensely moving experience to be reunited with many dear friends who had been my constant companions during that pre-Royal Ballet era. The sense of community and deep affection for each other has endured and strengthened over the years and our memories are still a living part of all our lives. Listening to Monica's inspiring speech, I felt not so much a 'has-been', but a tiny part of the foundation upon which Dame Ninette de Valois built her vision of a national ballet of international standard. Without 'Madam's' passion, faith and unshakable determination we would not have had the tremendous opportunities which her unique talent has opened up for countless dancers over three quarters of a century. And yet it is through every dancer who has come and gone that the vision has come alive and dances on into the future. I can't help feeling proud to be one of them.

Chapter Six

GISELLE and FIRST SEASON
at the ROYAL OPERA HOUSE

At the end of August 1957, when the Company reassembled after the summer break, we still bore the name of Sadler's Wells Theatre Ballet. However, plans and preparations for our graduation to the Royal Ballet Touring Company were already in place. We plunged straight into a three-week period of intensive rehearsals for the forthcoming tour and our first season at the Royal Opera House. These mainly took place, not, as in the past, at Sadler's Wells Theatre, but in the large company studio at the School in Talgarth Road. It was strange to be back at the school as a company member, and mingle with students starting out on the same road as I had done four years ago. In some ways it felt like yesterday, but now I was in the completely different world of a professional dancer which focussed around the theatre. The Opera House now became that focus: for individual coaching sessions in its small studios, costume fittings and relaxation in the large and comfortable green room. The underground journey from Baron's Court to Covent Garden became an integral part of my life, as did negotiating the lorries, basket-bearing porters and wooden crates of London's main fruit and vegetable market on the walk from Floral Street to the stage door.

I learned that I would dance *Giselle,* for the first time, at the opening week of the tour at Streatham Hill Theatre, but what I did not know at the time, was that if my performance met with Dame Ninette's approval, I would dance the role at the Touring Company's first season at the Opera House in January. I think I might have died of fright if I had been aware of Madam's intention; it was intimidating enough to be informed that the great lady wanted to coach me personally for my first ballerina role.

Unfortunately, before I had even put a foot into the studio, I incurred Madam's wrath. Not imagining that I would become a principal dancer so soon, I had had my hair cut into a fashionable bob. It was easy to attach a hairpiece, when a classical style was required and conceal the join under one's headdress, but this would not be acceptable as a leading dancer. I tried to conceal my short hair by wearing a scarf at all times, but one morning, while drinking a cup of coffee in the Opera House 'green room', Madam surprised me. As she snatched the scarf off my head and all eyes focussed upon me my shame was intense. Then, breaking a pin-dropping silence, the well-known voice rang out in outrage: 'I will not have one of my ballerinas with short hair, grow it at once, Alexander!' My only grain of comfort was that I had been referred to as a 'ballerina'.

The one-to-one coaching sessions for *Giselle* with Dame Ninette, in one of the tiny Covent Garden studios, were the most valuable training any dancer could wish for but they were also extremely nerve-wracking. I knew my career was on a knife edge and I could be dismissed at any moment. Often I feared the worst when my attempts to master the huge challenges of the role (which is regarded as the *Hamlet* of ballet, demanding a brilliant technique and a high

Rehearsing for Giselle

64

degree of dramatic skill), failed to please. Madam would turn her face away in disgust exclaiming, 'I can't look at you Alexander.' Then, stalking to the door, she would look back over her shoulder, casting a glimmer of hope into my dejection with, 'I will see you tomorrow at the same time.'

I had twenty four hours in which to master the impossible. The famous first act solo concluded with a series of complicated pirouettes which stretched me beyond my known limits, but it was the choreography of the second act adage that completely defeated me. A slow promenade in arabesque, where I was supposed to pivot on the spot without a hint of a wobble, was followed by a smooth, graceful plié, from which I was required to ascend effortlessly into the air, execute a faultless entrechat six (beating the feet across each other three times with lightning speed) and alight 'with the grace and softness of thistledown' with perfect balance intact. I then had to stand on one leg again with the other extended on a level with my armpit, all the time maintaining an air of serene composure and the unearthly lightness of a spirit.

Next morning, warming up in the little studio, with my offending hair hidden under a wide elastic headband, I prepared for Madam's arrival with trepidation. I had just about mastered the entrechat six, but the thistledown landing was still beyond my capabilities. Nor could I prevent my square shoulders from rising in tension while I struggled to hold my balance and I am sure my facial expression was far from serene. However, there were moments when pure joy burst through and something must have convinced Dame Ninette I was worth all the hard work and attention she was giving me.

My partner, who took the role of Prince Albrecht, was Alexander Bennett. His handsome dignity was ideally suited to the romantic style of *Giselle* and *Les Sylphides,* the next duo we would perform together later on in the tour. Rehearsals for the pas de deux in both ballets were taken by our director, John Field, who was himself a former principal dancer in Ninette de Valois' original company. Anne Heaton, the leading ballerina of Sadler's Wells Theatre Ballet at that time, would often come to our rehearsals and I learned much from her experience and help.

Finally, the day of my first performance arrived on 11 September 1957. At a Wednesday matinee performance at Streatham Hill Theatre, I followed in the original footsteps of Carlotta Grisi for whom *Giselle* was created one hundred and sixteen years ago. But it was not this Italian ballerina, (about whom I had learned only through books) who opened my heart to role, but the incomparable Galina Ulanova. Although the memory of her exquisite performance, seen in September1956 when the Bolshoi Ballet first came to London, had left an indelible mark in my mind, it was my heart which had been profoundly affected. The passionate Russian ballerina had danced straight from her own heart and touched previously unknown depths in mine. When I opened the door of *Giselle's* cottage and took my first step onto the stage, I forgot everything I had been taught and a feeling of intense joy swelled up in my heart. I could feel the peasant girl's delirious happiness in her inborn love of dancing. *Giselle* danced as a bird flies and despite dire warnings from her mother about the danger of overtaxing her weak heart, she could not constrain this integral part of her nature. I felt and still feel the same instinctive urge to express myself through my dancing body. The moment I stepped onto the stage at Streatham Hill Theatre my own being seemed to become one with that of *Giselle*.

I felt her happiness increase during the tender wooing of the mysterious young man with whom she has fallen in love. She has no idea that Albrecht is not the humble peasant he appears to be and I felt her opening herself to him in utter trust. Her ecstasy reaches its climax when she dances for him and her friends. I felt pure joy in the arch of my back, the lift of my head and the tips of my outstretched fingers. My whole being seemed perfectly poised on the arched point of one toe in a glorious moment when body, mind and spirit were in total harmony. For a split second I lost all consciousness of anything

"The arch of my back, the lift of my head".

outside that extraordinary joy which transcended even that of being in love.

Only now do I begin to understand what I experienced in that magic moment. I believe, when joy is detached from any dependence on another person or outside circumstances, it transcends the restrictions of time and we are given a fleeting glimpse of its eternal quality. It comes uninvited, unexpected and perches within our heart like a bird on the branch of a tree. We are honoured by its presence and when it flies away we are left with something immeasurably precious which will stay with us forever. The magic moment of that first *Giselle* lives on inside me now.

For me the tragedy of the ballet lies deeper than the Prince's betrayal, and when his true identity is cruelly revealed he shatters the vulnerable core of *Giselle's* being and in her desolation she tries desperately to reconnect herself to the source of her joy: dancing. I felt her frantic despair when she attempts to relive her dance of ecstasy, but her body stumbles out of control and crumbles into a void where only pain exists. She loses herself as I lost myself in swirling darkness which obscures the anguished faces of mother, lover and friends, and finally sucks her down into death.

I found the second act, with the terrifying adage, much more difficult. *Giselle* is transformed into a wraith-like spirit after her death and comes under the power of the Queen of the Willis. The Queen and her followers have all been victims of unrequited love and untimely death. They seek revenge on any unsuspecting male who ventures into the haunted woods at night. *Giselle* resists the power of the Willis and her love for Albrecht is restored when she realises his grief and remorse is genuine. The Queen tries to use dance as a weapon through which to exhaust and destroy Albrecht but Giselle's love of dancing and love of Albrecht merge into a greater power which transcends both and saves him from death. In the final moments, when the exhausted prince lies helpless in *Giselle's* arms, I felt her tender forgiveness swell up inside me as Adolphe Adam's emotive music reaches a poignant climax. At the first light of dawn, as the spirit of his beloved glides slowly back into her woodland grave, Albrecht suddenly realises she is gone forever and the curtain comes down on his sad, solitary, figure.

My second performance of *Giselle* took place the following Wednesday afternoon and Anne Heaton danced the role in the evening. But I was in for a shock when we reached Southsea the next week. An old ankle injury of Anne's flared up unexpectedly and she was rushed off to London for an emergency operation. Mr Field asked me if I would dance both performances on the 25 September. My attempts to build up stamina over the past months stood me in good stead and at the evening performance a capacity house at the King's Theatre gave me a wonderful ovation. In the audience were my big brother, and his wife Jane, with whom I was staying for the week, as David was a captain in the Royal Marines and was currently stationed at Portsmouth. What no-one in the audience, and few in the company, knew was that the ballerina on the stage had been involved in a very un-ballerina like episode that afternoon.

After the matinee performance, I was resting in the dressing room I shared with Anne Heaton and her Siamese cat, when there was a knock at the door. It was Michael Boulton, who had come to invite me to go for a run in his new car. I declined, saying I should preserve all my energy for the evening and prepare myself for the second performance. A little break would do me good, Michael suggested, promising he would just take me 'around the block.' I weakly gave in to his persuasion, but insisted I must be back in fifteen minutes. I went just as I was, apart from exchanging my dressing gown for sweater and trousers, and climbed into the impressive Volvo Estate car in full stage make-up and an old pair of ballet shoes. Michael drove down a quiet rural road and after five minutes we stopped to look at the view. A few deep breaths of country air were enough for me and very soon I was anxious to return to the theatre. Michael, keeping to his promise, immediately turned on the ignition to start the engine.

Nothing happened! Dismay, bewilderment, then horror struck as he realised the brand new vehicle had run out of petrol. I began to panic. There was no telephone box in sight to call for a taxi, and to make matters worse we discovered that neither of us had any money on us. Then, just in time to prevent me from bursting into tears, help arrived in the form of a double-decker bus. Michael hailed the driver to stop and, very politely, asked an old lady sitting in the front seat if she would be kind enough to pay my fare. Although my made-up face and shabby ballet shoes attracted a few curious glances, no one said a word. Perhaps they felt sorry for the poor dancer who could not even afford her bus fare, but without the unquestioning generosity of my fellow passenger, I might have had a long and very uncomfortable walk back to the theatre.

Now that I was a fully fledged principal, my weekly pay had risen to fourteen pounds and I was rapidly increasing my repertoire. Alexander Bennett and I danced the leading roles in *Les Sylphides* in Bristol at the beginning of October and shortly after that I took the main part of Swanhilda in Ivanov's *Coppélia*. The latter was to become one of my favourite roles. Donald Britton, another Scot, was a wonderful Franz, and his strength and experience gave me confidence. Soon I felt relaxed enough to enter fully into the light-hearted fun of this popular ballet and the infectious melodies of composer, Delibes, were a joy to dance to. I particularly enjoyed the second act when Swanhilda and her mischievous friends break into Dr Coppélius's workshop. The naughty girl dresses up in the clothes of the toymaker's masterpiece (the life-sized doll, Coppélia), and fools the old man into believing she has come alive. Swanhilda is elated at the success of her prank and her unmerciful teasing reaches its height as she rips the pages from the doctor's book of magic spells. This act of vandalism shocked my young niece when her mother brought her to see my performance in Edinburgh. Aunty Susie had a fair bit of explaining to do to get out of that one!

The tour concluded in Hull at the end of November but I had one more engagement to fulfil before returning to London. Donald MacLeary had asked me to partner him in an extract from *Les Sylphides* in his home town of Inverness. The event was a special charity performance at the tiny Empire Theatre with a mixed p rogramme of solo acts. I readily agreed and after our last performance in Hull we caught the overnight train to Glasgow. Arriving very early next morning, we planned to fly to Inverness to give ourselves plenty of time to rest and prepare for the evening performance. Unfortunately the Scottish weather intervened. On reaching Glasgow Airport we were informed that Inverness was fog bound and the small, light aircraft had been diverted to Wick, Britain's most northerly airport. This was unwelcome news, but we had no choice but to climb wearily on board.

The next problem was how to make the journey from Wick to Inverness. Trains were infrequent and apparently non-existent at weekends. Our only hope, we were told, was the postman who would make the journey back to Inverness after his daily deliveries. This good man, ignoring the Royal Mail notice displayed on the door of his van, stating that no unauthorised passengers were permitted, offered to give us a lift. There were no seats in the back of the little vehicle but we followed the example of the other passengers and made ourselves comfortable on top of the mail bags, 'Postie' obviously ran a regular service in this remote area where public transport was scarce. He frequently stopped to pick up waiting shoppers or farmers with business in Wick, and as we left the town behind and hit the open road these grateful people were dropped off at lonely lanes leading to their isolated homesteads. Soon Donald and I had the back of the van to ourselves and were able to stretch out and ease our stiff bodies a little. Sleep was impossible. The road was narrow and bumpy and at the end of the one hundred mile journey we hardly felt in a fit state to dance at the evening performance.

But perform we did. Donald's family, who met us at the Inverness Royal Mail depot on arrival, whisked away their travel-weary son and

Coppélia

his bleary-eyed companion to their warm and welcoming home. Hot baths, hot food and tea, laced with just a very wee tot of whisky worked wonders. My memory of the show is a little hazy, but with such a famous and charming Highlander as my partner, I am sure it was a great success. My gallant sister, Ismay and husband, Ben, nobly drove up from Edinburgh to add their support and took me home with them at the end of one of the longest days of my life.

After a brief break, preparations for the Royal Ballet Touring

Waiting behind Donald Britton to be presented to the Queen Mother in Belfast.

Taxing Task For Ballet Deputy

A Giselle to command attention

SIMPLICITY KEY TO DANCER'S TRIUMPH

By ERNEST BRADBURY

IN the final estimate, one supposes, "Giselle" is the dancer's "Lear." The one is undanceable as the other is unactable—at least as either work is seen i the mind's eye. But attacks on both works will continue while man (and woman) have artistic aspirations; the difference here is that "Lear" demands the seasoned actor, the ripe and experienced man of the theatre. Giselle is the role of a young and innocent girl; and by the time any ballerina can acquire half the technique and stage experience for the part she is bound to have lost some of her youth.

A new Giselle was seen at Leeds Grand Theatre last night, the 21-year-old Susan Alexander, who is already, one understands, a white

INJURY to Anne Heaton, prima ballerina of the Royal Ballet's second company, caused Susan Alexander to dance "Giselle"—considered the most taxing of ballet roles—twice at Southsea yesterday.

The 21-year-old girl from Edinburgh had danced "Giselle" only twice before at matinee performances elsewhere on tour.

She was given an ovation by a capacity house at the King's Theatre, Southsea, last night.

The largest audience of the Royal Ballet's week at the theatre was seeing the 116-year-old ballet performed for the first time in Portsmouth.

Meanwhile, Anne Heaton was at a London clinic, recovering from a manipulative operation on her ankle.

"MINOR OPERATION"

Mr. Peter Higgin (Royal Ballet Business Manager) said last night that an old injury to Miss Heaton's right ankle had recurred and became acute during her dancing class on Wednesday.

"She was taken to a Harley Street specialist and had a minor operation."

He said Miss Heaton's ankle was operated upon at one o'clock yesterday afternoon, soon after her arrival at the clinic.

"We hope she will be able to dance on Friday," he added.

Tonight's programme is a repeat of Tuesday's, when Miss Heaton danced the long leading roles of "Fete Etrange" and "Blood Wedding."

Afterwards she expressed a preference for tragic or "vaguely pathetic" roles.

The change of plans also put Miss Alexander's partner, Alexander Bennett, to a double test, matinee and evening performances.

He earned a warm reception from the large audience for his dancing in the exacting role of Count Albrecht, condemned to dance until he dies of exhaustion, though he survives.

LEADING ROLE

Miss Alexander is to dance the leading role in "Les Sylphides" in Bristol next week, and, says Mr. Higgin, she is soon to dance the lead in "Coppelia."

Making a brief appearance in "Giselle," Donald Britton displayed the verve and dancing skill that made him the leading man of this touring company.

His partner in the pas de deux was Brenda Bolton who won everyone's heart as "Solitaire," the title character of the ballet which preceded "Giselle."

Audrey Farriss was a cute

SUSAN ALEXANDER

The Girl on her toes to-night

I WENT to see Susan Alexander because I had been told that she is the bright new hope of The Royal Ballet Company — a young ballerina on the threshold of what promises to be a great career.

There is nothing about 21-year-old Susan to distinguish her from hundreds of other well-bred girls who share a Kensington mews flat with a couple of girl friends.

In the quiet tidy sitting room filled with reproduction Regency there was not a hint of grease paint or a ballet shoe.

Susan poured out coffee, looking in cashmere cardigan and well-cut tweed skirt every inch the daughter of a well-to-do county family. Which she is.

A BATH FULL OF PRAISES

Bouquets—in the bath

SO many and so little space.

A STAR IS BORN

London applauds Susan's triumph

Oh what a hap-hap-happy day it was yesterday for 21-year-old Susan Alexander from Edinburgh.

Susan was to have danced two minor roles in the Royal Ballet's second company production of "Giselle."

BUT INSTEAD SHE WAS THE STAR.

For 80 minutes yesterday afternoon she held the audience at a London theatre spellbound as she danced one of the most difficult roles in classical ballet.

Susan's big chance came because Dame Ninette de Valois, director of the Royal Ballet, saw her do a solo dance.

She gave instructions that this girl from the chorus was to be trained for the part of Giselle.

Susan made the grade—and yesterday her mother, Mrs. Margaret Alexander, of 38 Garscube Terrace, Murrayfield, saw her daughter's triumph.

The manager of the Royal Ballet said last night—"This is a terrific performance for such a young dancer."

Before she left for a celebration dinner with her mother Susan said—"My chief worry was that I might lose my wig—but it stayed on, thank goodness."

Susan started dancing with 2s 6d a week lessons in Edinburgh when she was nine. Then she went to a ballet school in Surrey and three years ago joined Sadler's Wells.

She lives with four other girls in a London flat and in her spare time makes clothes.

"There's no time for romance," she said. "Life is too full of dancing."

Susan will be in Scotland soon.

A STAR IS BORN

She's Susan Alexander, 21-year-old Scottish dancer. She danced Giselle at the Covent Garden ballet last night, and News Chronicle ballet critic Elizabeth Frank says: "I felt an absolute certainty of being present at the birth of a star."

—and this girl has greatness in her

By ELIZABETH FRANK

GISELLE—COVENT GARDEN

THERE have not been many occasions when I have felt an absolute certainty of being present at the birth of a ballet star.

Last night's new Giselle emerged to me as a complete and wonderful surprise.

Susan Alexander is a Scot and she is just 21. She still has the round, chubby face of a child and she retains something of a child's wonder in all she does.

I am more than happy to eat my words of a week ago, when I wrote of "a surfeit of 'Giselles'."

Sudden tears

Miss Alexander made me cry in this ballet, for the first time for many years.

In the opening scene she showed that particular quality of joyous youth which I remember in Fonteyn's first "Giselle," nearly 20 years ago. And in the mad scene, she created something all her own —a kind of touching bewilderment and real anguish which, added to her youth, brought sudden tears to the eyes.

In her dancing, she has a strong, individual style; beautiful, high-arched feet, reminiscent of Pavlova's; a strong musicality and superb balance.

Perhaps most amazing of all was her calm, serene assurance when one remembered that here was a young, untried girl making her debut at Covent Garden in one of the greatest of classic roles.

Yet there was nothing academic about her performance. Each movement of arm or head, the almost triumphant arch of her back in arabesque—all that she did, in fact—seemed part of a complete emotion.

Susan Alexander is not just another young artist of talent, she is—I sincerely believe—a great ballerina in the making.

Susan ... a Sinatra fan

New star of ballet takes her turn at the chores

By ELIZABETH FRANK

THE little Scots girl, Susan Alexander, who was cheered at Covent Garden as the youngest Giselle to make her debut there, was doing her Sunday chores when I called on her. "It's my turn to clear up," she said, putting away dustpan and brush.

The small mews flat in Kensington which she shares with two other Royal Ballet dancers, was like a conservatory with the 10 bouquets the new star received on Friday, her first night.

Although Susan, now 21, has been with the junior company for nearly four years she has been a principal only since last September.

hobbies

Susan has no hobbies. "I haven't time, what with rehearsals, class and housework, and now I have to write 18 Thank you letters for all the flowers and telegrams."

Although through all her working life she hears only the music of the classical composers, Susan is a staunch Sinatra fan and loves swing music.

Her first ambition was to dance Giselle. "I never dreamed that it would be my first leading role," she said.

Alexander's Dramatic Dancing

In the evening Susan Alexander and Alexander Bennett danced the principal roles. She brought a sort of soubrette charm to her dancing of Giselle. This practical girl should shrug away the betrayal by Albrecht and settle down to marriage with Hilarion.

She danced her first act variation with happy skill — full of zest, and unshadowed by impending events.

Because of this "no-nonsense" approach, her mad scene came with baffling suddenness and made impact by sheer dramatics and not by emotion. In Act II her "Will" was a modest girl, not a disturbing revenant, but she danced extremely well and looked like a lithograph of the period.

A Giselle to Touch the Heart

By DUNCAN HARRISON

THE Junior Royal Ballet's latest Giselle, Susan Alexander, made an impressive start to her first appearance in the great testing role at Covent Garden last night. She has youth and prettiness, flexible sensitive feet, grace of arms, and sound technique.

In her Mad Scene Miss Alexander achieved more than some fully fledged ballerinas: she touched our hearts. And not only was her pathos penetrating but she gave the role dramatic depth.

SUNDAY DISPATCH

Company's all-important debut at the Opera House began in earnest. The season opened on 26 December and daily rehearsals continued until Christmas Eve. There was no time to go home, so I spent Christmas day with David and Jane in Portsmouth travelling up to London early next morning. Our programme included three new ballets by young British choreographers. Kenneth Macmillan's *The Burrow*, was a disturbing and dramatic work based on the *Diary of Anne Frank*. It caused a sensation and introduced the extraordinary talent of the young Canadian dancer, Lynn Seymour. Peter Wright's *Blue Rose* was considered a 'promising start' and John Crank's *The Angels*, a bold experiment. Dame Ninette took a keen interest in every aspect of the productions. Peter Wright had created a solo part for me in *Blue Rose,* and Yolanda Sonaband was the designer of some highly original sets and costumes. The Opera House wardrobe mistress had serious misgivings about the latter. At a fitting of my cunningly swathed pale yellow tunic, an argument between choreographer,

Coppélia. Partnered by Donald McLeary.

designer and wardrobe mistress raged over my head. I stood like a tailor's dummy, in bra and tights, while Yolanda draped pieces of flimsy organza over my body in a vain attempt to convince the seamstress that the cloth could be cut and sewn in the manner of her ingenious design. Finally Peter, in frustration, went to Madam's office to seek her help. Striding into the dressing room, she immediately took charge of the situation and with her customary directness, briskly asked: 'Now, what's the problem?' Peter explained, showing Madam Yolanda's sketch. The wardrobe mistress said it was impossible to follow, implying she did not think the designer had a clue about dressmaking or how to cut fabric on the cross. 'Nonsense!' Dame Ninette exclaimed, grabbing the pin cushion and peering at the sketch simultaneously. Within minutes she had pinned and draped the yellow organza onto my bra and tights and created almost an exact replica of the design. 'Simple,' said Madam, turning me round to indicate the mastery of her work, 'Now get on with it.' Problem solved.

In his critique of the London season, James Monahan attributes the 'special quality of well-schooled and animated gaiety' of the young company to Madam's 'indomitable powers of leadership'. Her constant presence infused a heightened sense of apprehensive excitement in the lead up to this crucial season which, if we were considered worthy, would determine our future as an integral part of Britain's Royal Ballet. With the senior company already established and currently dancing to great acclaim in America, it was now up to us to prove we could hold the London audience in their absence. I am sure 'Madam' believed we could, but her faith in our ability was an awesome responsibility.

I will never forget, standing on the vast and well-worn stage of the Opera House on Saturday, 10 January 1958. In a few minutes the curtain would rise on *Giselle*. Several dancers were making last moment adjustments to shoes, checking their entrances and practising difficult steps 'just one last time'. I had reached the point where there was nothing more I could do but compose myself and pray that I would not fail the company or Dame Ninette. 'Beginners' had been called, the orchestra was tuning up, the chatter of the audience was quietening then 'Madam' walked on stage to wish us luck. She looked worried. 'Show me your pirouettes, Alexander,' she commanded. With sinking heart I obeyed but fluffed the troublesome sequence which concluded my solo. With the 'I cannot look at you' expression on her face, 'Madam' shrugged and left me to my fate. Not a very propitious start.

But by the end of the overture I felt nothing mattered but the present moment and the memory of Ulanova, perhaps standing on the same spot as I stood now and dancing on the very stage I was about to enter, worked its magic. As the music got nearer and nearer to those three little knocks on the cottage door which I knew were made by my beloved, so my heart rose in excitement and I stepped out of the dark wings into a glorious world of light. *Giselle* took over, as she always did, and I felt so completely inside my body that there was the same extraordinary fusion of spirit and flesh I had experienced at my first performance. An incredible sense of freedom filled me and I was able to execute the 'difficult bits' with new confidence.

When the huge, heavy red velvet curtain descended at the end of the ballet, and the audience broke into enthusiastic applause, Alex and I hugged each other with joy. The curtain rose and fell, rose and fell as the company took call after call. Then the bewigged flunkey in his traditional costume held aside the central flap for the principals to take their solo bows. Alex and I stepped through together and faced the crowded auditorium as so many world famous artists have done over the ages. And then the magic moment came when I stepped through alone. How tiny I must have seemed, as Galina Ulanova had seemed when I was one of the ecstatic people who applauded and shouted her praise fifteen months ago. But now it was my turn to stand in the spotlight and be showered with flowers. I had never felt so happy in all my life.

Suddenly I seemed to have shot to stardom. It was a phenomenon which took me completely by surprise and one that I can only now put into context. The 'junior Royal Ballet's' debut was, according to Joan Lawson's report for the Vic Wells Association, 'an absolute justification of Dame Ninette's policy' and 'an immensely successful visit to the Royal Opera House'. She goes on to commend the company for 'achieving the impossible' in producing three new ballets on the previous twelve-week provincial tour, describing how word spread like wildfire that this was a company to see, not just for its high standard but for its potential. The excitement of seeing new works and dancers who displayed 'conspicuous talent' would have mounted during the three week season and by the time I, a complete unknown from the ranks, made my debut as the youngest Giselle to dance the role at the Opera House, I imagine the atmosphere was electric. I was extraordinarily lucky to be in the right place at the right time, doing the right thing.

After a celebration dinner with my entire family, who had all come to watch my performance, I returned to the Earl's Court flat with my sister Anne. Her husband Martin had nobly volunteered to stay at home in Wakefield and look after the baby. Anne wanted to make the most of her 'night off' and insisted we should stay up until the newspapers came out the following morning. I was far too exhilarated to sleep and was happy to spend the night talking to my sister. It was quite like old times in our shared bedroom on the top floor of our childhood home. At five o'clock Anne ran round the corner to the news-stand by Earl's Court Tube station and came back laden with copies of all the main Sunday papers. Feverishly, we tore through the pages to the arts section and were confronted with;

'A STAR IS BORN', 'this girl has greatness in her', London applauds Susan's triumph' and **'A Giselle to touch the heart'.**

Anne and I hugged each other ecstatically and then proceeded to study the small print. Elizabeth Frank said: 'I felt an absolute certainty of being present at the birth of a star.' and confessed I made her cry.

Another critic spoke of 'the remarkable poignant intensity of grief brought to the mad scene' and 'yet she retains something of a child's wonder in all she does'. Almost without exception, the critiques continued in this vain. And it didn't stop there. The next day the phone rang repeatedly and press photographers besieged the flat. I was snapped, apron on, doing the chores, washing up and pretending to cook. The numerous bouquets got a headline all of their own, '**A BATH FULL OF PRAISES**'. Then there were the usual questions about marriage and falling in love and I gave my customary reply that I hoped it would not happen for a long time as I believed marriage and ballet would not mix; besides I had no time for boyfriends and there was nothing else I would rather do than dance!

I was brought back to earth on Monday morning. The Royal Ballet Touring Company was opening in Brighton that evening and there was a train to catch. We were all elated and encouraged by our success in London but we would be 'on the road', without a break, until our next visit to the Covent Garden Opera House in July. Meanwhile we continued to work towards new productions, simultaneously giving eight performances a week in eighteen different venues. There was a very important tour to prepare for in the autumn. We would be one of the first professional British companies to travel to the other side of the world to perform in Australia and New Zealand. In 1958 this really was considered to be 'the back of beyond'.

Chapter Seven

AUSTRALIA and NEW ZEALAND

The Royal Ballet Touring Company set off into the unknown at the end of August 1958. Our destination was Sydney, Australia. The Empire Theatre had been booked for an eight-week season but the management had not been able to arrange accommodation for the company of sixty-two dancers, orchestral musicians, stage crew and members of staff. We had been asked to fend for ourselves as best we could.

Fifty years ago the Sydney Opera House was not even a twinkle in Australia's architectural eye and visitors from the Northern Hemisphere were rare. Communications were primitive by today's standards and trying to make contact with 'the other side of the world' was a lengthy and unreliable business. We really were travelling into uncharted territory. The journey, on a DC 7 aircraft, took three days. We flew for ten hours, then, when the plane ran out of fuel, it seemed to drop out of the sky and land on whatever part of the world happened to be underneath. I remember staggering out into oven-like heat at various times of night and day, (time had lost all meaning) and following the person in front of me across the burning tarmac. We then had one hour to spend in a hot, dusty lizard-infested waiting room of somewhere like Jakarta, about whose existence my geography teacher had failed to inform me. This procedure was repeated twice more, until later, thirty six hours since leaving London, we reached Sydney.

I had managed to procure somewhere to stay, through the friend of a neighbour's second cousin who knew a family in Sydney with a spare room to rent. With the address in hand, I hailed a taxi and lay back in the cab, too exhausted to take an interest in where I was being taken, but wearily wondering what my digs would be like. At least the Australians spoke English and I wouldn't have to struggle with French, Spanish or German, but my top priority was a comfortable bed. The taxi finally delivered me to a large suburban villa on the outskirts of town, with a rambling garden leading down to a little sandy beach on the banks of a river. This was to become my refuge and haven over the next two months.

Work started almost immediately. Every morning, after a delicious breakfast of fresh pineapple, pawpaws and mangoes, I caught the bus into Sydney for the ten o'clock company class and every evening, after five or six hours of rehearsals, I made the same forty-minute journey back to my digs. All I wanted to do was eat and sleep but my boisterous Australian hosts made this difficult. The family of four constantly seemed engaged in rowdy tennis parties, followed by rowdy barbecues and then, when the sun went down, rowdy television viewing. I resisted all attempts to persuade me to join in 'the fun' and, at the risk of appearing unfriendly, escaped to my riverside retreat whenever I could. At this point in my life, I began to think deeply about Nature's power to restore an inner sense of peace and perspective. I wrote poems, expressing my instinct to withdraw from the 'madding crowd' and reconnect myself to the uncontaminated energy of all life which I sensed flowing in the river. The solace I felt in these solitary reveries gave me the same harmony that I felt in my body, in those rare magic moments, when every nerve and cell seemed united in perfect alignment. Sitting quietly by the sparkling water, I had my first glimpse of understanding in an eternal quality, which not only came alive when I danced, but resided within me when I was still.

The season opened at the Empire Theatre on 11 September with *Coppélia,* Rowena Jackson and Philip Chatfield taking the leading roles. As the week progressed our programmes included more challenging and contemporary works, like *Hamlet, Rake's Progress* and *Pineapple Poll,* but the Sydney audiences' reception was cool. We were obviously going to have to prove, once again, that we deserved our Royal status. The only British ballerina whose fame had so far reached this remote part of the world, was Margot Fonteyn. Although she would join us later on in the tour, her presence was sorely missed in Sydney. However, we were determined to win these sceptical people over and gave of our best night after sweltering night. By the end of the first month, we were playing to packed houses at every performance and had earned high praise from both the public and press. Our reputation for the rest of the tour was now secured.

Sundays were spent on Sydney's famous Bondi Beach. As in South Africa in 1954, caution was thrown to the wind and we indulged in unlimited sun and warm seas. I bought my first bikini, but the strength of the Australian sun was an unknown entity and, like many members of the company, I became badly sunburnt. My midriff was soon bright pink and very sore, not a good idea for any ballet dancer who is constantly gripped in that area by her partner. I was now learning the leading role in *Swan Lake* which, being full of high lifts and supported pirouettes, caused rehearsals to be agonising. When I peeled my leotard and tights off my skin peeled too, and the dressing room floor seemed to be strewn with Lux soap flakes. In our revealing costumes, we girls had to apply lashings of 'wet white' to disguise red necks and arms. Very soon, my bikini was discarded and visits to the beach were curtailed to the moonlight swims after the Saturday evening's performance.

A highlight of my time in Sydney came when I received a telephone call from Canberra. My father had written to an old flame who was now married to the Governor of Australia, Sir Bill Slim. He and Lady Aileen kindly invited me to spend a weekend with them and John Field equally kindly gave me permission to accept. I thought I had better look smart and hastily purchased a little white hat and matching gloves. I flew to the capital city on a Saturday morning (having been given the day off), and was met at the tiny airport by a young man in military uniform. He was curt, but as I noticed a small appliance stuck into his ear, I assumed he was deaf and made allowances. He remained silent, as he drove the official black saloon to Government House, except for the occasional muttered remark which sounded a bit like, 'a hundred and thirty not out'. I didn't like to say anything to this odd person and wondered if he was suffering from something more serious than deafness. I was beginning to feel a little nervous about the weekend but on arrival at a palatial white mansion, I was greeted by a smiling Lady Slim. She immediately made me warmly welcome and showed me to a beautiful bedroom overlooking the garden. I was invited to make myself at home and come down to the blue drawing room for cocktails at six o'clock. I could understand why my father had been attracted to this charming lady and Sir Bill was just as delightful. I sat next to him at dinner and he engaged me in animated conversation until ten o'clock when he left the table, saying 'Please excuse me, Susan, I am afraid I have to go and govern Australia!' The wonderful weekend in Canberra gave me a taste of what lay ahead.

News of our hard earned success preceded us to the elegant city of Melbourne and we were welcomed like truly Royal visitors, with a reception in the gardens of Government House given by Sir Henry and Lady May Abel Smith and Princess Alice, Countess of Athlone.

Dress was formal, so white gloves were hastily bought and those who had hats wore them. The opening night at Her Majesty's Theatre on November 10 was attended by their 'excellencies' and the whole of Melbourne high society turned out in their finery. The atmosphere was a complete contrast to the initial weeks in Australia and took us by surprise. We were inundated with invitations to a variety of events including a day at the races at the Melbourne 'Ascot', a Sunday picnic party and, best of all, a grand Christmas ball at Government House. Fortunately, we had been advised to bring evening wear and the ruched white dress I had bought for the marvellous farewell party my father had given for me at the Savoy Hotel, on the eve of the eight-month tour, would be just the thing. I decided it needed some improvisation for such a prestigious occasion on 20 December. Des, the wardrobe master was inundated with requests from us girls to help us create 'Cinderella' ball gowns out of our relatively modest, English-style outfits. Excitement mounted as the great night approached; treats like this were rare in the Touring Company's life and we were determined to make the most of it. As soon as the curtain came down on the Saturday evening performance there was a flurry of activity in all the girls' dressing rooms. Stage make-up and false eyelashes were hastily removed, hair vigorously brushed out from restrictive classical styles and pink tights replaced with nylon stockings. The wardrobe department was overwhelmed with last minute requests to put a tuck there or pin a strap here and the ever-helpful Des swathed a floral silk drape onto my dress and sewed me into it moments before a fleet of limousines drew up outside the stage door. I never gave a thought about how I would get out of it after the ball was over.

My thoughts were focused on the dashing young aide-de-camp who seemed to have taken a fancy to me at the garden party. Champagne flowed, delicious food was provided in abundance, the band played all my favourite dance tunes, and my handsome escort swirled me round the floor again and again. I was in a romantic haze. It was only when I staggered back to the rented house I was sharing with several other dancers, that the spell was broken. Like Cinderella, my beautiful ball gown had to be dismantled, but trying to cut my way out of Des's creation at three o'clock in the morning was beyond me. I collapsed onto my bed and a deep champagne-induced sleep immediately engulfed me. When I woke, with sore head and sore feet, my crumpled white dress and silk swathe seemed to have been reduced to a ragged memory of its former glory and I noticed the heel of one of my gold evening sandals was broken.

Christmas was a strange experience in Australia. I and a few fellow members of the Company were invited to a swimming party in the grounds of one of Melbourne's grand houses. As we sat under green umbrellas around the large pool, full Christmas dinner was served. Roast turkey and plum pudding seemed inappropriate on what felt like a summer's day, but, not wanting to offend our hosts, we did justice to the feast. I think we were all a little bit homesick and the atmosphere was subdued. It would be a relief to get back to work.

'Work' now reached a particularly exciting stage. Two of the Royal Ballet's greatest stars, Dame Margot Fonteyn and Robert Helpman, had flown out from England to join us and Dame Margot was going to coach Lynn Seymour, Donald MacLeary, Christopher Gable and myself for *Swan Lake*. We had been practising the roles of Odette/Odile and Prince Siegfried since the beginning of the tour and now it was time for the 'fine tuning'. We felt immensely privileged to have Britain's greatest ballerina as our coach and not a little apprehensive. But Dame Margot was a gentle teacher and soon put us at our ease. *Swan Lake* is one of the toughest tests in the classical repertoire. As well as considerable technical challenges, including the notorious thirty-two *fouéttes* in Act III, the 'Jekyll and Hyde' role of the Swan Princess demands strong contrasts of style and interpretation. While Lynn and Donald danced their parts before our teacher's meticulous eye, Christopher and I practised discreetly behind them. And then it would be our turn to be put through our paces. Dame Margot's coaching was an inspiration to me, giving a

Dancing and dining with the dashing young aide-de-camp.

unique insight into the delicate details of the role and the total dedication which this experienced ballerina brought to everything she did. I saw how she approached the role with true humility and immersed herself in the spirit of the ballet, allowing Tchaikovsky's beautiful music to guide all her movements. In deep gratitude for all she had done for us, we novices gave our inspiring mentor a bouquet of flowers. Dame Margot's thank you note is still one of my most treasured possessions.

Lynn and Donald gave their first performance of *Swan Lake* in Melbourne. Lynn was only nineteen and was the new 'white hope' of the Royal Ballet. Her exceptional fluidity, beautiful soft arms and highly arched feet were ideally suited to the bewitched Swan Princess. Both she and Donald went on to have long and celebrated careers as dancers and Christopher eventually branched out into teaching, directing and acting. I followed a different path but at that time the future looked rosy for us all. I made my debut as the Swan Queen on 15 January 1959 in Adelaide. Although technically stronger and more experienced than Lynn, I could not compete with her exquisite portrayal of Odette, the white swan, but my Odile (the wicked black swan in the ballroom scene), was described as 'a real flashing-eyed coquette' and my thirty-two fouettes gained a spontaneous round of applause. In hindsight, my own view is that I was less successful in the strongly lyrical style of the lakeside acts and had not yet penetrated the meaning beneath the fairy tale. However, Dame Ninette wrote to say she was 'happy to hear such good reports of my

first "*Lac*", commenting that it was 'a mouthful of a ballet to tackle.' I would certainly agree with that!

Adelaide was unbearably hot. We found it almost impossible to sleep and, in the hope of finding a breath of air, we moved our mattresses out onto the balcony. But in the squat suburban villa (rented for the month) there seemed to be no air at all. The only way to cool off in the middle of those suffocating nights was to have a cold shower and lie down again while still sopping wet. The theatre, like our rented accommodation, had no air conditioning back stage, and it was as difficult to keep your make-up from running into your eyes as it was to squash swollen feet into tight, narrow, pointe shoes.

However, our plight paled into insignificance when news of a disastrous bush fire hit the city. The lord mayor of Adelaide launched a Relief Appeal and the Royal Ballet offered to give a special midnight performance in aid of the appeal. Arrangements were rushed, as the company was leaving Adelaide the next day, but a programme which included *Les Patineurs, Rake's Progress* and *Coppélia* Act III was hastily devised. I was proud to dance Swanhilda in the latter with Robert Helpman as Dr Coppelius. The great Australian star had a busy night as he also played the demanding role of the Rake in Ninette de Valois' challenging ballet. The evening was a resounding success and was attended by the UK Commissioner, Lord Carrington, with Lady Carrington, the Governor, Sir Robert George and his entourage. The vice-regal party was welcomed at the Theatre Royal by an RAF guard of honour. I now begin to understand why my brother David was included in a press report about my first performance of Swan Lake; the fact that I was the sister of an equerry to Prince Philip was considered to be of equal, if not more importance, to the loyal subjects of Adelaide in the nineteen fifties.

Brisbane was even hotter than Adelaide. We were accommodated in a small city flat but were horrified to find the place infested with cockroaches. They crept out of tea packets, lurked in dark corners in the bathroom and snuggled up in the ash tray on my bedside table.

Dame Margot's thank you note.

When we complained, Robert Helpman, being born and bred in this climate, explained these unwelcome creatures were part of life here and there was nothing we could do except get used to sharing the flat with them. We tried, but not without the greatest difficulty. Now, as

Debut as the Swan Queen

well as the heat, our nights were disturbed by ominous rustling noises and, every night, when I returned home after the performance, I found my bedroom floor covered in slumbering cockroaches. I did not dare get into bed for fear of treading on one of the wretched things. Eventually, I solved the problem. Before entering, I put my hand round the bedroom door, keeping my eyes closed, then switching on the light and singing loudly in order not to hear the beasties rushing to hide under the bed, I took a flying leap onto the bed, hopefully without touching the floor. Finally, pulling the mosquito net over my head, I managed to convince myself that if I could neither see nor hear the intruders; they must be more frightened than I.

At the end of February we left Brisbane (with an element of relief) and flew to New Zealand for the last lap of this marathon tour. There were five blessed free days before opening night on March 4 in Dunedin. Donald MacLeary, Alan Beale and I decided to hire a car and do some exploring. Although both Donald and I had driving licences, lack of practice made us somewhat unreliable at the wheel, but Alan was very understanding. Fortunately there was little traffic to contend with and as soon as we left town the roads were virtually deserted. The stunning scenery of New Zealand's South Island and the freshness of the crystal-clear air lifted our spirits. The classic beauty of the snow-capped Southern Alps and vast, sparkling lakes reminded me of a magnified version of the Scottish Highlands. I thought at the time this was the only place I could imagine myself living other than my beloved homeland, although I had to admit the climate was a great deal better. The three of us played like children on wide, white beaches, paddled in frothy blue seas, picnicked in the hills and found somewhere to eat and spend the night when darkness fell. It was wonderful to be young and free and to enjoy the uncomplicated friendships which now seem one of the greatest and lasting blessings of my time with the ballet company. We loved to dance, we loved life and we were held together by a deep affection for each other. There were times in my later life when I thought I had lost those blessings but, as I write, I understand that they were not lost, just hidden for a little while.

Feeling refreshed from the idyllic little holiday, we returned to Dunedin ready to go. Accommodation had, once again, been impossible to arrange. The Company manager had had to advertise in the local paper, requesting the good folk of Dunedin to squeeze us into their homes. For me, it was a squeeze indeed, as I found myself sharing a room with a ballet-mad teenage girl. Every night I would be confronted with a pile of autograph books to sign for her schoolfriends and, not content with that, my 'room mate' would continue to ply me with questions, ignoring my attempts to get some sleep. But I was much more fortunate than my friend, Valerie Reece who, in desperation, spent the first night sleeping in a skip at the theatre!

We were all relieved to move on to Christchurch after only three days in Dunedin. By this time, a few telephone calls had been made and more suitable, but unmemorable, accommodation had been found for the following two weeks. But when we reached the North Island we were once again forced to throw ourselves on the mercy of the local population. All I can remember about Wellington is that it lived up to its name and was extremely windy.

The final fortnight in Auckland turned out to be one of the best times of the whole eight months. A charming English couple offered Lynn Seymour, Margaret Lee and me hospitality in their delightful and spacious home. Dr and Mrs Goodfellow's generosity as hosts and the homely atmosphere into which they welcomed us still remains a precious memory. Breakfast on the balcony overlooking the beautiful garden, a cosy Sunday relaxing in the comfort of deep, soft armchairs and, when the sun went down and an evening chill descended, a bright fire bringing a warm glow into the room. Such are the simple pleasures which brought the comfort and solace we needed after the long and arduous tour. It was time to go home.

Chapter Eight

SLEEPING BEAUTY and an
ENCOUNTER in MANCHESTER

Life was soon back to normal and in May 1959, the Touring Company set off on a trip to the familiar towns of Bournemouth, Cardiff, Birmingham and Southsea. The story of my 'two Giselles in one day' in September 1957 seemed to have entered Southsea's local folklore and still got a mention in the press. I had gained strength and experience since then and had on more than one occasion surpassed that feat. I had once danced six major roles in one day: the pas de deux in Les *Sylphides,* the Girl in *Solitaire* and Blanche in *Pineapple Poll* at both the matinee and evening performances. I was not 'a plucky wee Scot' for nothing! However, I have to admit that I was looking forward to the annual month's holiday with special eagerness. The gruelling routine and constant challenges of provincial touring were even more demanding since becoming a principal but there are some 'disasters' which, in retrospect, have a funny side. Once, at the end of *Giselle,* Act II, as I glided tragically back to my 'grave' (a trapdoor, operated from below by a stage hand, down which I was supposed to mysteriously disappear) I miscalculated the spot. My sorrowful farewell to the grieving Prince Albrecht was becoming unbearably prolonged and I could not understand why I was not descending below stage as usual. It was my prince, Alexander Bennett, who spotted the problem and came to my rescue. All the while, keeping his face composed in sorrowful expression, he whispered through barely moving lips, 'move about a foot to your left'. Then I too maintaining the countenance of the unearthly waif, managed to float to the correct spot and consequently disappear as designed.

Another similar occasion occurred at the end of *Swan Lake.* In this ballet, heroine and hero are united in death and during the final apotheosis are seen floating into the ethereal distance on the back of a giant swan. This cunning contraption, looking graceful and romantic from the auditorium, was attached to a strong wire which in turn was attached to a bicycle wheel hidden behind the wings. The idea was that by winding the wire gradually around the wheel, the swan 'carriage' would glide smoothly across the back of the stage and fade from view as the music reached its poignant climax. Unfortunately, not all stage hands were practised wire-winders and once, somewhere on tour, my final journey as Swan Princess was distinctly bumpy and my prince and I traversed in a series of ungainly jerks! Poor Sid, the stage hand, was distraught but all was forgiven over a pint in the pub after the show and a good laugh.

Waiting at home in Edinburgh, was a little car of my very own. During the Australian/New Zealand tour I had, for the first time, been able to save some money. With a little financial assistance from my grandmother and the co-operation of my father, I had managed to purchase a white Morris Minor with a maroon convertible roof. I felt I had 'arrived' and imagined myself looking like the film star, Audrey Hepburn with smart dark glasses and a shocking pink headscarf over my (now long) hair. I christened the car 'Toushka'. She would give me a new freedom on tour to drive from place to place and no longer have to endure those tedious Sunday train journeys. The first major journey Toushka and I were to make was from Edinburgh to London at the end of the holidays. I contacted my co-driver of New Zealand, Donald MacLeary, and invited him to accompany me. Yes, he said, he would be delighted, agreeing to come down from Inverness to Edinburgh by train the night before we set off. We planned our epic trip with meticulous care, obtaining a route map from the AA, and booking an overnight stop at my sister Anne's, in Cheshire. She and Martin, with their growing family, now lived in a two storey cottage and were, as always, happy to give hospitality to me and my friends.

Excluding this welcome break, the whole drive to London took the best part of two days, with many stops to consult the map and check we were going in the right direction. The old A1 was primitive by the standard of today's motorways and my little car shuddered at fifty miles an hour, but our sense of freedom and achievement was great. Life on the road was going to be much more fun from now on.

The Royal Ballet Touring Company's third season at the Royal Opera House opened on August 17. The success of the season was Lynn Seymour's and Donald MacLeary's London debut in *Swan Lake*. I was now, at the ripe old age of twenty-three and a half, established as one of the Touring Company's ballerinas and no longer held the unique allure of new talent. I had danced the leading roles in Coppélia with Donald Britton several times but when I saw my name on the cast list for *Giselle* I was filled with awe and trepidation. Although I had matured my interpretation and improved my technique, I think James Monahan was right to wonder (in January 1958) whether, 'ever again she will so thoroughly enchant an audience?' Performing at the Opera house was always an honour and a challenge but nothing ever surpassed the magic of my debut. I was just lucky enough to have been chosen by Madam to dance the role of *Giselle* at such a special time and to ride on the crest of a wave

93

Solitaire *with Donald MacLeary*

created by the whole company at our first Royal season. I will always feel immensely privileged to have been one of Dame Ninette's dancers and to have had the invaluable benefit of her personal attention and encouragement.

I can vividly recall 'Madam's' magnetic presence on the stage at the dress rehearsal of my next ballerina role, *Sleeping Beauty*. Beryl Grey, whose Princess Aurora I had watched so closely when playing the part of a Royal page in my student days, was also there. Now I was learning the nuances of the role from this great ballerina who was one of the stars of the original Sadler's Wells Ballet. Since the Royal 'merger', principal dancers from the senior company often performed with the Touring Company as part of Dame Ninette's growing policy of free exchange of artists, ballets and choreographers. Despite the formidable technical feats 'Beauty' presented, I adored this ballet from the start. I felt more at ease in this role than that of the Swan Princess and there were moments of pure joy when I could totally abandon myself into the power of Tchaikovsky's glorious music. I can still hear and feel the mounting excitement in the introduction to Aurora's first entrance, when she bursts into a dance of untrammelled youthful happiness. It was impossible not to be swept into the carefree mood of the music even although in minutes, you were about to plunge straight into the fiendishly difficult 'Rose Adagio'. The famous courtship dance of the princess and her four suitors culminates with a series of promenades and balances on the point of one toe. When the balances 'came off', I felt an intense exhilaration which I know was shared by the audience. When they were not so good, then the four noble suitors could be relied upon to steady me up and hopefully the audience didn't notice.

For *Sleeping Beauty*, I was honoured to have a Prince of great experience and stature, Desmond Doyle. The relationship between a ballerina and her partner is unique. To build an intuitive blending of movements and bodies requires total trust in each other. I can think of no other situation when two people come into such intimate contact, physically, mentally and emotionally and yet retain a degree of respect which keeps the relationship pure. Perhaps actors or musicians share this experience but, when your body is the instrument of expression, you give your whole self to the other and at times become one entity. Off stage, relationships between company members retained this special intimacy and deep respect which remain unique in my experience. There was often real love, free from any sexual expectation, which for me, still a remarkably naïve and immature young woman who had not even menstruated at the age of twenty-three, was and is something immeasurably precious.

Sleeping Beauty was special. For no other ballet, did I take such care in selecting my pointe shoes. Weeks before an impending 'Beauty' I laid aside any shoes of promise. These were then worked into exactly the right degree of softness, with enough stiffness still left to give the required support. New pointe shoes made much too much noise to be used on stage until 'worn in', under socks in class, or even bashed on concrete steps until they became virtually silent to wear. We used the expensive satin shoe ribbons (which we had to buy for ourselves) time and time again, unpicking them from worn out shoes before carefully washing and ironing them so they could be sewn onto a new pair. The ribbons, tightly bound around our ankles with a double knot tucked invisibly into the groove behind the inner ankle bone, secured shoe to foot but in order to keep the tight fitting satin slippers from slipping off our heels, we girls used a mixture of spit and resin which formed a kind of glue with which we smothered the canvas lining. The boys, who did not have ribbons on their leather 'flatties' used 'Copydex' much to the wardrobe staff's despair as it ruined their tights. Both boys and girls wore jockstraps for different reasons: the former for comfort and appearance and the latter to prevent the pink tights from wrinkling. I would yank the precious hose up to my armpits then tuck the top under two corset-tight bands of thick broad elastic where I hoped it would not budge until I took them off at the end of a performance. To this day, I have dark marks on the skin covering my hip bones!

The 'balance' shoe for the Rose Adagio was crucial and when my personally made batch of shoes arrived, from Frederick Freed's famous London shop, I searched through to find the ones with the flattest points. The best from these was then marked 'B. act 1 R' and, when the time came, would clad my right foot in the first act of 'Beauty.' I had specially marked ones for acts II and III as well; soft for the vision scene where a nymph-like quality is essential, and firm for the wedding and finale to sustain the rigours of the grand pas de deux with the nerve-wracking 'fish dives' and the whirling coda. There is a series of flying leaps in the glorious coda into which I poured all the unfettered joy I felt when I danced on the beach in North East Scotland during my school holidays. I abandoned my whole self into the leaps, all my flesh and blood gathered into the air with a burst of energy which seemed to explode from the core of my being. Then, for a split second, I felt I was held still and motionless,

Princess Aurora in Sleeping Beauty

balanced in a timeless moment of ecstasy when I was weightless and knew I could fly.

In November 1959, the Company performed at Manchester Opera House for a week. I was staying with Anne and Martin in their cottage at the Cheshire village of Prestbury. Now, with my own transport, I was free from dependency on local bus services and the twenty mile drive to Manchester was easily manageable. It so happened that a public school friend of Martin's was in Manchester on business the same week as the Royal Ballet and was staying at the Grand Hotel.

Another pose for Sleeping Beauty

My sister was determined to introduce me to this eligible young man and John was duly invited to Oak Tree Cottage, at a time when I 'just happened' to be free. He, in turn, invited me to have dinner at his hotel on my night off. This was a completely new experience for me and, although flattered and excited, I also felt a degree of anxiety. I even telephoned my mother to ask her what I should do if I needed to go to the loo. 'Just say you want to powder your nose, Susie.' Ma made it sound simple, but John obviously had no idea that under my sophisticated appearance was a nervous and inexperienced girl.

The night after dinner in the Grand Hotel, I danced *Swan Lake* with Alexander Bennett. I was back in the world I knew and loved, dancing the fairy tale love story with a Prince of such noble tenderness that, as in *Giselle,* my heart opened fearlessly to his love. I was beginning to feel more at ease with the 'white acts', especially the poignant final scene where Odette is comforted by her swan maidens after the evil magician Rothbart had thwarted Prince Siegfried's attempt to rescue her. Tchaikovsky's heart-rending music moved me deeply and, with all the major technical challenges of the previous acts behind me, my body relaxed and melted in sympathy. At the end of the performance I was presented with a large bouquet from the successful young business man staying in the Grand Hotel. His world was far apart from mine and completely unknown to me, and yet, in less than a year I would leave my world and enter his.

John was very persistent, and red roses (from Moyes and Stevens, one of London's top florists) began to appear regularly at every curtain call. I got used to and began to enjoy the luxury of candlelit dinners in expensive restaurants and soon I was faced with the unavoidable question of marriage. John wanted us to get engaged, which, according to the conventions of those days was a binding commitment. The idea simultaneously attracted and frightened me, and I knew it was what both my family and John's expected. The security of a home was certainly alluring after years of living out of a suitcase and I certainly wanted to have children eventually; but it would be a wrench to give up my career and leave the family of dancers who had come to mean so much to me. I stalled and said I would give John an answer after the forthcoming three month tour to South Africa, but in my heart I knew what it would have to be.

Chapter Nine

SOUTH AFRICA REVISTED
and FAREWELL PERFORMANCE

A week after the Royal Ballet gave the final performance of their seventeen-week provincial tour at the Gaumont Theatre, Southampton they flew to South Africa arriving at Johannesburg on 31 January 1960. The Company was greeted by almost a thousand people at Jan Smuts Airport eager to catch a glimpse of the dancers. First to step out of the plane were three ballerinas, Svetlana Beriosova, Antoinette Sibley and Susan Alexander, all in smart attire as befitted the occasion. I wore a natty little tartan suit with matching beret to live up to the name I proudly bore, 'the Scottish girl'. When I remembered the company's modest arrival at Cape Town docks six years ago, and my lowly position as the most junior member, it dawned on me that both Sadler's Wells Theatre ballet and I had come a long way since then. Now we were a truly integrated part of the Royal Ballet and would soon be joined by two more senior ballerinas from London, Beryl Grey and Nadia Nerina.

First to welcome us was Mr Alec Gorshel, the mayor of Johannesburg and Mr Stodel representing African Theatres. Then we were let loose among a throng of press photographers and radio interviewers. Desmond Doyle, a native of South Africa attracted particular interest and was met by his former dancing teacher and his brother, Monty. But there was another Cape Town born male principal, who had been banned from coming on this tour because of the colour of his skin. Johaar Mosoval's presence was sorely missed by the whole company especially when we visited his home town later in the tour. Apartheid was still in force and coloured people were barred from entering the theatres but the growing unrest against this cruel and unfair system was on the point of eruption.

We had three days to settle into the new climate and prepare for the opening night at the Empire Theatre on February 5. Svetlana was quoted as saying: 'muscles move much more easily in the heat' and was undaunted by the high altitude having danced in Denver, Colorado, which is even higher than Johannesburg. But for some of us, with less experience, this proved a problem. On my first performance of *Sleeping Beauty* I made an all too realistic collapse at the end of the first act when the princess pricks her finger. When the curtain fell I was helped, breathless and dizzy, into wings. The theatre management had thoughtfully provided an oxygen cylinder for just such an emergency, and after a couple of whiffs I felt fit enough to carry on without further mishap. The respected Johannesburg art critic, Dora Sowden, reported that: 'of the three Princess Auroras, Nadia Nerina was the most enchanting,' Svetlana Beriosova, 'the most elegant and exciting,' and so 'deft and dainty was Susan Alexander at the afternoon matinee, that she had the young members of the audience applauding at every step'. The Prince Florimunds, David Blair, Donald MacLeary and Desmond Doyle, were praised for bravura, aristocratic nobility, immaculate partnering, and Donald got a special mention for his 'shining solo'.

Having fun with Graham Usher 'Moo'.

I felt hugely privileged to share the principal dressing room with Nadia and Svetlana and, as with all the principals from the 'main' Royal Ballet Company whom I still viewed with some awe, they treated me as an equal. Antoinette Sibley, a little younger than me, was a rising talent and our names were often linked with those of Lynn Seymour and Merle Park as the stars of the future. Few knew of my impending engagement and for the time being, dancing was still, by far, the most important part of my life. However, in respect to my would-be fiancé and to protect myself from the attentions of other men, I came to an arrangement with my very good friend, Graham Usher. 'Moo', (as he was always known), had left his partner, Petrus, behind in London and the two of us decided we would pretend that we were a couple. I loved Moo dearly in the pure, platonic way of many company relationships, and having such a delightful escort made the receptions and parties with which we were feted, much more fun. Donald MacLeary was another close friend and a photograph of the three of us dancing the Charleston, captures the spirit of those happy days.

The people of Johannesburg were eager to entertain us and one wealthy family invited Donald, Svetlana, Moo and me to make free use of their house, garden and swimming pool. Whenever we had a few hours off we would lounge on deckchairs around the tree-shaded pool, slipping into the dreamy blue water to cool off every now and then. A little maid in white cap and apron refreshed us at regular intervals with gooseberry ice cream and long, iced drinks of unusual pastel colours. A small child, Maluli, daughter of the house, sometimes came to chat but mostly we were left by our generous hosts to enjoy the peace of their beautiful garden without interruption. I cannot remember the names of these wonderfully understanding people whose kindness knew no bounds. Donald and I were even entrusted with their Cadillac and they urged us to make use of it whenever we wanted. The vast limousine was a far cry from my tiny Morris Minor and parking in town was a challenge. I left that particular exercise to Donald but got out of the car to guide him with elaborate hand signals. Our mime skills were further tested when it came to locking the vehicle. It proved not to be a simple case of turning the key in the car doors and neither of us could work out how to achieve the task. Finally we resorted to pretence, though whether any potential thieves were fooled by our act of 'checking' each door with loud cries of, 'All right your side, darling?' we will never know.

The harsh reality of the two opposing sides of South African life was brought home to us with the shocking shooting incident at the native township of Sharpeville. Angry crowds protested outside the theatre at the vicious colour ban which forbade their right to see our performances. We all felt the terrible injustice of this and suddenly the world of swimming pools, Cadillacs and bouquets seemed hollow. The atmosphere in our hotel was filled with tension, and many of the

African waiters and maids were absent. Those who remained to serve us were silent and grave. My heart went out to them. We felt increasingly uncomfortable and feared our presence was making the situation worse. The company wanted to demonstrate our own opposition to apartheid and the loss of one of our most valuable soloists due to the brutality of this law. Plans to give a special performance for the coloured population were urgently discussed and would come to fruition when we reached Cape Town in April.

On March 20 the Royal Ballet travelled to Pietermaritzburg to give two performances at the Grand Theatre. My memory tells me there was nothing very grand about this small, country town, which seemed to be a stark contrast to the bustling busy city atmosphere of Johannesburg. The audience was, I imagine, mostly drawn from the surrounding farms and for many this was their first opportunity to see a professional company from overseas. We were very much on show during this tour and conscious of the reputation it was our responsibility to uphold. Even when 'relaxing' on the lawn of our hotel, the dress code required the standard expected by our 'Royal' status, with suits and ties for the boys and high heels and stockings for us girls.

The tour progressed to Durban where we were welcomed back by many who remembered our visit six years ago. The two-week season was a predictable success, but it was the final season in Cape Town that was most memorable. The undoubted highlight was the Royal Ballet's special performance to one thousand coloured people at the City Hall. The entire Mosoval family attended the matinee but the absence of Johaar had never been felt so acutely. The programme consisted of exciting extracts of all the ballets in our repertoire 'brought out and presented at their best.' When the curtain went up in the grand hall there was an audible gasp of wonder as Beryl Grey and Bryan Ashbridge opened the performance with the ethereal *Sylphides* pas de deux. When it finished a tiny girl dressed in a frilly pink party dress, climbed up onto the stage to present the ballerina with a sheaf of flowers and the audience roared its applause. This was a real community occasion when the dancers were as much inspired and moved by the spectators as the spectators were by the rare opportunity to see professional ballet. I danced one of my favourite pieces, *Don Quixote,* with Donald Britton. The dramatic pas de deux was followed by virtuoso solos for both the male and female dancers. With scarlet tutu and black fan, I felt a real *femme fatale* and relished the sultry music and sensuality of my solo. Donald's vivaciousness and strength always gave me confidence and added to the exuberance of the fiery finale. At the end, Johaar Mosoval's' little sister, Moegmina, presented me with a beautiful bouquet and I felt a lump rising in my throat. The Royal Ballet gave their final performance in Cape Town at the Alhambra Theatre, on April 30 and although the auditorium reverberated with rapturous applause, nothing could surpass the unique atmosphere of the momentous afternoon at City Hall.

Now, with my last major tour completed, I had passed the test which gained the right to that coveted title of 'ballerina' and my salary had reached the dizzy heights of twenty pounds a week, but the honour and privileges, joy and love, were the real treasures of being part of this wonderful company of dancers which I would leave in just four weeks' time.

When the plane touched down at London airport on May 1, I knew my engagement to John Pretty would be formally announced in *The Times* five days later and I was about to descend into a fait accompli situation. Standing at the top of the gangway, with Moo by my side, I turned to my dearest friend to whom I had come so close, and said, 'I'm shit scared, Moo'. He squeezed my hand and replied with the words of encouragement we always gave to each other before stepping onto the stage, 'Atta girl Sue'. I let go of Moo's hand and slowly walked down the steps to greet my fiancé waiting on the tarmac below.

I was immediately swept into preparations for marriage. My

parents had already been in discussion with John while I was in South Africa and the wedding date was fixed for August 6. Soon I was immersed in a world of bridesmaids, hymn sheets and dressmaker's fittings. I began to feel excited about my new role and moving into the company director's smart house where my husband-to-be was already living. A real home of my own seemed very alluring after so much travelling. But there was still a little more to do before I left the stage and 'settled down'.

The Royal Ballet had a three week trip to Ireland planned and opened in Dublin on May 16. My mother, father and my Aunt Mattie came from Scotland and booked into the Hibernian Hotel in order to attend some of their daughter's last performances but all the talk was about my forthcoming wedding. It seems extraordinary that no one, not even I, foresaw the trauma that such a sudden departure from my life of dance would cause. The whirlwind romance was like a fairy tale and when John came for the weekend and sent me a bunch of red roses to complement my ruby engagement ring, I imagined marriage would bring the 'happy ever after' ending I had been led to believe.

The Dublin audiences gave us their customary enthusiastic welcome and Donald Britton and I were given a glowing write-up for *Coppélia*. The critic said that seldom had he enjoyed this ballet more and the combination of 'charm, technique and engaging athleticism won the house'. The programme also included *Sleeping Beauty* which I danced on the Friday evening and again, due to Antoinette Sibley being off with an injury, the following Saturday afternoon. By the end of the second performance I was absolutely exhausted and felt I wouldn't mind if I never had to do another Rose Adagio in my life. It was at this moment that 'Madam' chose to visit the company and to my eternal regret, I voiced these feelings to her. Dame Ninette responded by inviting me to lunch at her hotel at the beginning of our second week in Dublin.

I was expecting a reprimand for my outburst, but instead, the great lady seemed to understand that my mind was no longer fully focussed on the ballet. Madam's kindly enquiries about my wedding dress and my new home took me by surprise. I saw a different side to the fierce coach and indomitable director, and the genuine interest she showed did not stop after I left the Royal Ballet Company. My gratitude expanded as I relaxed over a delicious lunch and I dared to ask Madam to come to my wedding. Dame Ninette said she would be delighted.

My final performance was at the Belfast Opera House on Saturday, 4 June 1960. A few nights before, I had been one of the principals to be presented to the Queen Mother and the governor of Northern Ireland. I did not realise that a party from Government House was once more in the theatre on Saturday night. It was *Coppélia* again, Donald and I had excelled ourselves and I was riding on a crest of elation. The whole company assembled at the end of the performance to bid me farewell and to give me a wedding present of a particularly frilly and flimsy negligee. I immediately donned the romantic garment and was parading around in a very flirtatious manner, when, taking me by complete surprise, John Field and the Governor walked onto the stage.

My hasty attempts to recover a dignified composure and execute a suitably reverent curtsey were greeted with gales of laughter. My last moments with the Royal Ballet and my family of the past seven years were filled with joy and I carried all their love and good wishes with me into the next chapter of my life.

EPILOGUE

Marriage did not bring the happiness I expected, and I felt lost and lonely in the director's house when my husband was out at work all day long. His life had not changed as mine had done and I did not know what to do with myself. The role of a wife was one I failed to master however hard I tried and my efforts to learn to cook and keep house seemed singularly unsuccessful. I missed my ballet friends dreadfully and mourned the loss of my life of dance. Even the joy the birth of my two lovely children brought me, did not fulfil something deep within my being and I felt guilty and inadequate.

It was my husband who, unwittingly, pointed out the source of my depression. One day, after another disaster in the kitchen, he sighed and said, 'Let's face it, you are only good at one thing. Why don't you get yourself a little job at the Royal Ballet School?' That was it! Now I knew what was the matter with me. I wasted no time in approaching Dame Ninette and as always Madam had the answer. Repertoire classes were being introduced into the curriculum of the junior school in Richmond Park in the autumn, she said, and would I be interested in teaching them? Would I? I was absolutely delighted to accept

Madam's invitation and immediately started giving myself a daily class, in our parquet-floored living room, while my daughter was at play group and my baby son asleep in his pram.

The Royal Ballet's most recent establishment, White Lodge, was situated in a former hunting lodge in Richmond Park. The residential school took children from the age of eleven and those who successfully completed the strict training graduated to the senior school as students. My job was to teach the dances from the ballets, which were still fresh in my mind and body, to the third year pupils. As soon as I started to dance again I was happy, and the joy of passing on my knowledge to the next generation filled my dark empty place with light. This new outlet for my passion was the start of a long and fulfilling teaching career in dance.

When the repertoire class at White Lodge was discontinued I decide to set up my own school of dancing. In 1967 The Royal Academy of Dancing invited Dame Margot Fonteyn to devise a brand

Marraige

new children's examination syllabus and organised a course for teachers to learn it. Once again I had the golden opportunity to be taught by the great ballerina who had coached me for *Swan Lake* and like Madam, Dame Margot encouraged me in my new career. I was learning different skills and began to appreciate the importance of a sound foundation of technique to underpin the soaring heights of dance.

The Susan Alexander School of Dancing opened in East Sheen Church Hall in September 1968 and for the next five years I encouraged many 'caterpillar babies' to unfold the butterfly within them. Even when the three-year-olds reached the age to be entered for the Royal Academy of dancing examinations, I urged them not to forget to stretch their colourful wings every now and then. When I became an examiner myself, I came to believe that 'the soaring heights of dance' were as important as technique and that every child has the capacity to fly, if only in their imagination. But without that imagination, dance can become a dull repetition of exercises and a meaningless technical display.

When my school, due to a change in my husband's job, was relocated to the Isle of Wight, I put my belief into practice. Realising how few of my pupils had seen any of the great ballets and how unlikely it was that they would ever have the opportunity to take part in them, I determined to rectify the situation. In 1980 I formed the Isle of Wight Ballet Company and every Saturday we forgot about the technique that we struggled with in the weekday classes. I recounted the magical stories of *Coppélia, Giselle, Swan Lake and Sleeping Beauty* to my eager students, encouraging them to act them out to recordings of the inspirational music. Suddenly, my own butterfly broke out of a chrysalis in which I had not realised it had been trapped. I saw that the creative urge within me, which was expressed through the medium of dance, was not restricted to the confines of a classical ballet dancer's body. These unsophisticated, and sometimes ungainly youngsters showed me the way to release my preconceived

Dame Ninette de Valois (Madam) at the wedding.

expectations of how a dancer should look and move and a new sense
of freedom filled the studio with joy.

I gave up examining and for the next five years concentrated on
my young ballet company. Of course, I still trained and entered my
pupils for the necessary examinations but now there was a purpose
to the exercises. I drew deeply on my experiences with the Royal
Ballet and the spirit of the Touring Company which had given me so
much and which I wanted to share with my pupils. I invited Lynn
Seymour and Donald McLeary to come to the Isle of Wight to be guest

111

teachers at our Summer School. Both my old friends gave inspiring classes and thanks to my famous colleagues my esteem rose favourably in my pupils' minds. Lynn was especially popular as, instead of teaching a solo from one of the many ballet roles she had performed to such wide acclaim, she donned a Hell's Angel T-shirt and taught a soft shoe shuffle. The former ballerina explained she was expanding her repertoire these days and exploring different styles of dance. Well fortified with cans of beer, which I had been asked to supply, Lynn's visit was a resounding success.

I now took on the roles of director and choreographer for the Isle of Wight Ballet Company, producing two shows a year. The classical repertoire included full-length productions of *Coppélia, Giselle* and *Sleeping Beauty, An Evocation of Swan Lake, Les Patineurs* and *Façade*. I also choreographed several original ballets, the most successful being *The Little Prince, Millers Damsel* and *Midsummer Night's Dream*. Choreography opened up new avenues of creativity and my world of dance began to broaden its horizons. In my search for new ideas, I began to read much more widely, developing an interest in poetry, art and stage design. I listened intently to concerts on the radio and bought a recording of anything which 'spoke to me', which I would play over and over again until I could visualise the piece in movement. Choreography, for me, became seeing music dancing.

But all of this was taking its toll. Finally my body gave up its increasing struggle to keep up with my flying spirit and collapsed just before my fiftieth birthday. My spine seized and I suffered a complete breakdown of health which confined me to bed for many months. For the first time, my lifeline of dance was severed and I was faced with the seemingly impossible task of trying to live without it.

Once again Dame Ninette de Valois, who had taught me how to overcome the insurmountable in my youth, came to my rescue. In February 1986, I was staying with friends in London while recovering from a week in hospital. It so happened that my visit coincided with an impromptu Gala at the Royal Opera House, hastily arranged to raise the necessary funds to prevent the threatened closure of Sadler's Wells Theatre. 'I've got to go,' I said, ignoring the perilous state of my health. My kind and understanding hosts managed to purchase three tickets for the evening performance and agreed to escort me to Covent Garden. As the programme opened with a wonderful display by the children of the Junior Royal Ballet School from White Lodge, I felt a familiar flicker in the deep core of my being. But there was more. I must have closed my eyes for suddenly I was aroused by the distant strains of Tchaikovsky's familiar music from the Rose Adagio. Was I dreaming?

When I opened my eyes I saw the stage was empty except for one elderly woman. Madam stood alone. Then, with all the stirring passion, determination and conviction I so well remembered, Dame Ninette gave a powerful speech about Sadler's Wells Theatre, the foundation upon which she had built the whole Royal Ballet. I sat up in my chair, feeling the faint flicker ignited by the passionate belief of this amazing lady. This was the quality beneath and beyond the individual dancers who come and go; this was the quality which would lead me into a new life when my body could no longer execute the steps; this was the quality which would keep my spirit dancing for ever.

And so it was. In time I recovered my strength and found new opportunities to express the creative source of my life in completely different ways. I thought that I could not live without dancing and there were times when I feared, like Giselle, I would die. But through working with colours and learning the ancient art of the spinning wheel, my body discovered an inner sense of balance. The fibres running through my hands seemed to weave a unique dance all of their own while the spinning wheel gathered them into a yarn of unique beauty.

I became fascinated with textile art and in 1988, following in my daughter's footsteps I went to India. In this amazing country I discovered the fabulous embroideries and patchworks of Gujerat which demonstrated the communicative power of folk to tell the ongoing story of ordinary people throughout the ages. This, and the Sarjan Centre of Creativity near Ahmedabad, where so-called 'poor' children expressed themselves through art, singing and dancing, made a profound impression upon me. These little boys and girls seemed so full of joy, energy and an inner strength which did not depend on any material wealth or social advantage. These little children would change my life irrevocably.

When I returned from my first trip to India a whole new way of living had opened up for me. Although my health was still precarious, I left the Isle of Wight for the east end of London where I started a textile project, which would eventually link children all over the world. The seven-year 'Rainbow Tree Project' resulted in an inspirational series of patchworks made for the Millennium, but that is another whole story about which I have written in another book.

Through the 'Rainbow Tree Project', I travelled widely and discovered a way to express myself in a completely new way. My body learned to tell its own story and I learned to listen to it. Together we learned to live in a more flexible and harmonious way in all sorts of challenging and unusual circumstances.

Eventually, I seemed to come full circle and returned to my roots in Scotland. I now live in the beautiful countryside of the Highlands and when I am walking in the hills or bathing in the sea I feel I am part of the dance of nature. The rhythm of the seasons and the music of the wind are the orchestras which inspire me and when I sit at my spinning wheel and blend the colours of the mountains and the vivid autumn trees I am at peace. But even when I sit in my garden, as still as a dewdrop on a rose leaf, the dance of my life is beating in the depths of my heart.

LIST OF ILLUSTRATIONS

115